STRINDBERG

STRINDBERG

An Introduction to his Life and Work

BY THE LATE

BRITA M. E. MORTENSEN

AND

BRIAN W. DOWNS

Emeritus Professor of Scandinavian Studies in the University of Cambridge

CAMBRIDGE

AT THE UNIVERSITY PRESS

1965

PUBLISHED BY
THE SYNDICS OF THE CAMBRIDGE UNIVERSITY PRESS

Bentley House, 200 Euston Road, London, N.W. 1
American Branch: 32 East 57th Street, New York, N.Y. 10022

First Edition 1949
First Paperback
Edition 1965

First printed in Great Britain at the University Press, Cambridge
Reprinted by offset-litho in the United States of America

CONTENTS

PREFACE

Our purpose has been, in this, the centenary year of Strindberg's birth, to furnish English readers with a brief introduction to his biography and to his main literary works and, at the same time, to indicate the directions in which those who wish to obtain a fuller knowledge might most profitably proceed.

B. W. Downs is responsible for Chapters I, II, III, IV, for the Bibliography and for the Index, B. M. E. Mortensen for Chapters V to IX inclusive, and for the Conclusion.

We wish to thank Messrs Bokförlaget Natur och Kultur for leave to reproduce the portrait, Messrs Bonnier of Stockholm for leave to reproduce the caricature on p. 89 and to refer to their edition of the Collected Works, and the Anglo-Swedish Literary Foundation, Messrs Jonathan Cape, and Peter Smith for permission to refer to the English translations. We also wish to thank A. H. J. Knight, M.A., the University's Director of Scandinavian Studies, Evelyn Downs and Helen Hoather for their encouragement, advice and practical assistance. No record of our grateful indebtedness would be complete if it did not include the names of Dr Martin Lamm, the *doyen* of researchers in the field into which we have ventured, and of Dr Torsten Eklund, who is carrying on his work in the great traditions of Swedish scholarship.

B. M. E. M.
B. W. D.

Cambridge

June 1949

LIST OF
STRINDBERG'S PRINCIPAL WORKS

BELOW is given a list of Strindberg's principal works, under the titles by which they are mentioned in this book, with the Swedish title equated in each instance. The arabic figures in brackets after the English title refer to the translations as given in the list on p. 225 below; the roman figures after the Swedish title refer to the volume containing the work in the *Samlade Skrifter* (55 vols. Stockholm 1911–21).

The Author = Författaren (XIX)
Black Banners = Svarta Fanor (XLI)
A Blue Book (20) = En Blå Bok (XLVI–XLVIII)
The Comrades (2, 3) = Kamraterna (XXIII)
Creditors (1, 3, 7) = Fordringsägare (XXIII)
The Dance of Death (1, 5) = Dödsdansen (XXXIV)
A Dream Play (1, 5) = Ett Drömspel (XXXVI)
Easter (2, 5, 13) = Påsk (XXXIII)
The Father (2, 5, 6) = Fadren (XXIII)
The Free-Thinker = Fritänkaren (I)
The Ghost Sonata (1, 5) = Spöksonaten (XLV)
The Gothic Rooms = Götiska Rummen (XL)
Gustavus Adolphus = Gustav Adolf (XXXII)
Gustavus Vasa (1, 5) = Gustav Vasa (XXXI)
Inferno (9) = Inferno (XXVIII)
In the Outer Skerries (12) = I Havsbandet (XXIV)
In the Red Room = I Röda Rummet (XIX)
Lady Julia (1, 2, 3, 5) = Fröken Julie (XXIII)
Legends (10) = Legender (XXVIII)
Lucky Peter's Journey (2, 5, 11) = Lycko-Pers Resa (IX)
A Madman's Defence (8) = En Dåres Försvarstal
    [Le Plaidoyer d'un Fou] (XXVI) [1]
Master Olof (4, 5) = Mäster Olof (II)

[1] Cf. p. 42.

CHAPTER I

THE LIFE, 1849–1872[1]

I

THE first and greatest of Strindberg's misfortunes was his birth. This took place at 8 o'clock on the morning of Monday, 22 January 1849 in a house, now demolished, on Riddarholmen Island in the city of Stockholm. At his baptism he received the Christian names Johan August. In his full-dress autobiographies he referred to himself as 'Johan'; otherwise 'August' was the only first name ever employed.

His mother, Ulrica Eleonora Strindberg, had borne her future husband three illegitimate children before her marriage to him in 1847. The daughter of a Stockholm tailor in a small way, Johan Olof Norling, and his wife, she had been first in service as a servant-girl and later as a waitress at a suburban tavern in Liljeholmen, and thence she had been taken, still quite young, in the autumn of 1843, to be the housekeeper and mistress of Carl Oscar Strindberg. Of the twelve children which

[1] A vast amount of material of all kinds is assembled in Martin Lamm's two big works, *Strindbergs Dramer* (2 vols. 1924–6) and *August Strindberg* (2 vols. 1940–2), and in J. Landqvist's appendices to each volume of the *Samlade Skrifter*. A small selection of Strindberg's large correspondence has been printed as *Från Fjärdingen till Blå Tornet* (ed. T. Eklund, 1946), and a much larger one, here quoted as *Brev*, is in course of publication (*August Strindbergs Brev*, ed. T. Eklund, Stockholm, 1948–). The most valuable general biographies are E. Hedén, *Strindberg, en ledtråd vid Studiet av hans Verk* (1921) and E. Castrén in vol. VII of H. Schück and K. Warburg's *Illustrerad Svensk Litteraturhistoria* (1932).

For the present chapter, besides the above-named, the reminiscences of two of Strindberg's sisters, A. v. Philp and N. Hartzell, *Strindbergs Systrar berätta* (1926), have been freely drawn on; the period of time covered is the same as in the first volume of the subject's autobiography, *The Son of the Bondwoman*.

they had in all, five died in their earliest infancy, and Ulrica Eleonora herself was carried off, by pulmonary consumption, before she was forty. Her photograph shows her to have had good looks, but suggests invincible stupidity. The consensus of her children's testimony attributes to her mildness, goodness, piety and open-handedness to the indigent, but, significantly, they make no reference to her competence as a housekeeper and mother. August, who attached uncommon importance to his heredity, represents her also as nervy and violent, and one medical writer [1] has assigned to her a specifically neurotic temperament which, he declares, was transmitted to her son August.[2] Certainly, her favourite child, a boy, appears to have been pathologically hysterical. She continued almost defiantly, it would seem, to regard herself as a member of the lower classes, consorting for preference with the servants in the house, and August maintained that she began to detest him as soon as he acquired Latin and Greek, the specific tokens of a better-class education. Something of this trait in her he believed himself to have inherited, and for that reason, in allusion to the story of Hagar and Ishmael,[3] he entitled his autobiography *The Son of the Bondwoman*.

Her husband, Carl Oscar Strindberg, carried on the business of steamship agent. Carl Oscar Strindberg's father, Zacharias, the son of a country clergyman descended from Ångermanland peasants, migrating to Stockholm towards the end of the eighteenth century, had set up as a grocer there and had married into the family of the joiner Neijber, a man of German stock.

---

[1] S. Rahmer in *August Strindberg, eine pathologische Studie* (1907), p. 36.

[2] He himself says, in *The Son of the Bondwoman*, with I know not what justification, that he was contaminated by his wet-nurse ('he had received from her inflammation in his blood, and cramp in his nerves').

[3] Genesis xxi. 13.

Zacharias cut something of a figure in the smaller *bour-geoisie* of the early century and wrote three short drama-tic sketches. His daughter became the third wife of Samuel Owen, an engineer of British birth and one of the promoters of steamship construction and navigation in Sweden. It was presumably through this connection that a steamship agency was added to the Strindberg grocery, subsequently separated from the original busi-ness and put under the charge of Carl Oscar.[1]

The latter, a sober, heavy, rather handsome and un-interesting man, who generally assumed, according to his son, the external imperturbability of the Icelander, led an outwardly tranquil existence revolving about his business and his home, never going into company or taking part in public entertainments. He had a fair-sized library, with the Swedish classics Wallin, Tegnér, Franzén and Frederika Bremer, encouraged the musical activities of his children and liked to hear Ludvig Strind-berg, a young nephew of his, an actor, talk about drama and the stage when he came to dinner on a Sunday. His retired mode of life may have been conditioned less by his temperament than by his circumstances—the com-paratively long co-habitation with a mistress, and that mistress's social shortcomings, which the legitimation of their union after four years could do nothing to remedy. Carl Oscar Strindberg, with his genteel proclivities, may well have felt himself to be *déclassé*,[2] forced to put up with a family life and a social life not quite worthy of him; such a sentiment would not make him an easy com-panion at home. He certainly kept himself to himself as much as the narrow circumstances of his household

[1] Nils Strindberg, a member of Andrée's polar expedition, whose pocket-diary provided a mystery in connection with its disastrous end, was first cousin once removed to Johan August.
[2] This is the view of M. Lamm, *August Strindberg*, I, 5.

permitted and was an object less of his children's affection
than of their respect and fear. 'Papa's coming' was the
signal for a general *sauve-qui-peut*.

With his parents, August's relations were unhappy.
From his mother, who, besides an exigent husband, had
so many children to look after, many of them weakly, he
did not receive all the affection for which he craved; it
remained in his memory that she 'could be unjust, violent, and punish unreasonably'. Between himself and
his father there seems from the start to have been a kind
of ingrained antipathy. In 1908, twenty years later than
his feverish autobiographies, August Strindberg wrote
in terms which strangely echo what Samuel Butler had
said about himself and Canon Butler: 'My father I always felt as a hostile force, and he could not bear me
either.' Like many unusual boys, August would dearly
have liked to impress his father, and this he utterly failed
to do. 'Nothing will ever come of him', was one of the
senior's disparaging remarks, and when he was told that
In Rome had been accepted for production at the Royal
Theatre—the first of his son's plays to be so distinguished—he uttered but one word: 'Fiasco.' Carl Oscar
Strindberg resolutely refused to take any interest in his
son's literary work and, what was as bad, gave him no
help of any kind in starting him in life.

It would be unjust to put all the blame for this calami-
tous state of things on the seniors. If August's mature
relationships are anything to go by, he may well as a
child have put impossible demands on his weak,
harassed mother's affections; and he had too many tem-
peramental weaknesses in common with his father for
even the best will in the world to avert perpetual fric-
tion. Both were in a high degree self-righteous, un-
sociable, self-willed and masterful; the erotic emotions

in both were uncommonly strongly developed; in both a burning core of violence could only be banked down in smouldering, sullen resentment; in rather different ways, both needed what cannot be otherwise described than as 'elbow room', and that their circumstances signally denied them.

Family relations were further strained when Ulrica Eleonora Strindberg died on 20 March 1862. A few months before this, a handsome young woman of twenty, Emilia Charlotta Petersson, the daughter of a sexton, was brought in to keep house in her place. Carl Oscar Strindberg perhaps paid Ulrica Eleonora an unconscious compliment by repeating his first matrimonial experiment and marrying Emilia Petersson as soon as decency allowed.

Many years later, when he was speculating about his heredity and about his ambivalent feelings towards women, Strindberg dwelt on his recollections of his mother, and the death-bed scenes were a shock to his nerves, but at the time of her death he cherished no very profound or sentimental feelings for her; accordingly he was not likely to resent, as children sometimes do, the introduction of another into her position and dignities. Greatly prone to jealousy in all its forms as he always was, however, it is possible that something obscure of this sort entered into his adolescent bosom: he might envy his father and also feel that his father's new love would lessen any chance of the affection for which he had vainly looked. Though spiritually inclined to pietism, the stepmother was pleasure-loving, and August, who for a short while saw in her an ally, at any rate as far as religion went, professed himself highly scandalised when he saw her dancing in a place of public resort. Suspicion clouded their relations; he certainly acquired no friend in her; and she raised a further barrier between himself and his father. One of his sisters declares: 'With August she never succeeded in establishing a confidential footing. Already as a child he was difficult to get on with. Shy and sensitive, he was at the same time very contrary, wanting to argue about everything great and small. With his defiant disposition and his deep-rooted suspicion of everything and everybody his relations with his step-mother soon became strained and gradually he looked upon her as his sworn foe. In this way he also incurred his father's displeasure, from which ensued perpetual disputes and quarrels.'[1]

Young August must have been an uncomfortable housemate. Brothers and sisters in later years were ready to make allowances for him, and for several years he was on intimate terms with his brother Axel,[2] but no warmth of affection, past or present, emanates from the family records. Unhappily for him, August's musical endowment was small, and so he was only imperfectly implicated in one of the household's few bonds of union, the evening concerts which they used to give in the common sitting-room. There is a photograph of him extant,[3] taken when he was sixteen years old, and showing him as well grown and rather striking than handsome. Mouth and chin are weak, and there is an air of uncertainty and somewhat sullen defiance about his uncommonly lofty forehead and his posture, which somehow raises the suspicion that he has been well whipped, but that the whipping has either been too much or too little.

[1] Philp, A. v. and Hartzell, N., *Strindbergs Systrar berätta*, p. 32.
[2] They are reflected in the relationship indicated between the Gentleman and his Brother in *The Storm*.
[3] Reproduced, for instance, in *Strindbergs Systrar berätta*, facing p. 14.

2

Carl Oscar Strindberg's business was subject to considerable vicissitudes of prosperity. August came into the world when his father's fortunes were at their lowest. He was on the very point of being declared insolvent, and, though he was to rehabilitate himself later, his bankruptcy on the one hand marked him with a stigma even more painful than that of the irregular union which he had recently legitimated, and, on the other hand, confined him for several years to the narrowest material circumstances. Between August's third and eighth years, his parents, their growing family of children and their two or three servant-girls—to whom by day was added Fru Strindberg's old mother—were confined to a three-roomed flat with room for nothing but the occupants, chairs, tables, beds, cradles and the malodorous washing of infants; and, to play in, the children had at the back the amenities of a dark, dank yard, full of rats, garbage-pails, earth-closets and other abominations.

The flat, situated on the second floor of a gaunt, over-populous house opposite both the churchyard of St Clara and the fire-station of Stockholm, remained associated in August Strindberg's mind not merely with domestic squalor, with fear of his father and with hunger —which his sister Nora puts down to a fastidious appetite rather than to actual shortness of provisions—but also with the dismal clanging of bells and the misfortunes of conflagration and of burial, to which his own family added more than its due quota, since five of his own brothers and sisters died in infancy. In 1856, Carl Oscar's fortunes having mended, this residence was exchanged for one further from the centre of the town, in

7

Norrtullsgatan.[1] The new home was certainly larger
and more comfortable; but it had its drawbacks: one of
its frequently changing owners was a butcher, who kept
ferocious dogs and carried on his business on the premises. Little wonder, even if Sue and Dickens added
their literary suggestions, that the frequent metropolitan
scenes in August Strindberg's plays and novels have a
nightmare-like quality, relieved by little of the humour
and none of the geniality of *Little Dorrit* or *The Old
Curiosity Shop*.

From 1856 onwards the younger members of the
Strindberg family spent their summer holidays in the
country. On a field-day with the volunteers towards the
end of his school days, August caught sight for the first
time of the sea and the archipelago of innumerable little
islands and skerries that guards the eastern approach to
Stockholm. He was entranced by it, and at all periods
of his life he was to have recourse to this *skärgård* for
refreshment to his body and imagination.

3

From a small dame's school, August Strindberg was
sent, at the age of seven, first to the preparatory department of St Clara's School (Klaraskola) and then to the
school itself. It was a public school and a notoriously
hard one. Flagellation was incessant, a form of disci-
pline to which the boy was well inured from home,
where his grandmother acted as whipper-in-ordinary to

[1] The Strindbergs lived at 14 Norrtullsgatan from April 1856 to April
1857, from April 1860 to October 1864 and from April 1867 to April
1869; they were at 12 Norrtullsgatan from October 1864 to April 1867
and from October 1871 to April 1873 and at 25 Gråbergsgatan (in the
suburbs of Stockholm) from April 1857 to April 1860 and from April
1869 to October 1871 (facsimile of Carl Oscar's diary in *Strindbergs Systrar
berätta*, facing p. 10).

the family, with father and mother to reinforce her feebler hand on more serious occasions. After a short interval (1860–1) at the Jakobs Skola, which may have been less barbarous but was definitely proletarian in its clientèle, he was placed in 1861 at the Stockholm Lyceum. This was a private establishment and, though based on the classical curriculum of the Germanic *gymnasium*, its teaching enjoyed the merited reputation of being advanced and humane as well as efficient. Here young Strindberg was at last able to develop his intellectual powers more freely, though he was not to show unusual promise as a scholar. In spite of weakness in mathematics and some aversion from the classics, he rose (for one term) to the top of his form; but he passed out of the school no higher than eighteenth out of twenty, his best marks being for Swedish, French, Natural History, History and Geography. This 'student-examen', entitling him to matriculate at a university, he passed apparently without undue luck or exertion in May 1867; and, in accordance with the custom of his country, he celebrated his success by getting ceremonially drunk.

4

The idea of proceeding to the University of Uppsala may well have originated at that epoch in August's religious development when he had thoughts of becoming a clergyman, probably at about the age of fifteen. His was a religious family. His father was known to read the sermons of Archbishop Wallin in leisure hours and liked his family to appear regularly in the family pew; but Carl Oscar Strindberg seems to have been content spiritually with the forms and formularies of the established Lutheran church. His two wives, on the other hand, were infected in some degree with that form of pietism, a striving after more individual and emotional holiness, which, under the nickname of '*läseri*', was fairly widespread in nineteenth-century Sweden and especially among the more reflective and self-respecting artisans, small shopkeepers and peasants. To this, for a time during his early days at the Lyceum, August too was so strongly given that at the age of fourteen or so he became notorious as a '*läsare*' among his schoolmates, haunted sermons and 'exercises' and believed his family to be destined for Hell through indulging in the mild pleasure of an excursion on Sunday afternoon.

His first fervour, however, did not last. When, in April 1865, the time came for his confirmation, he seems, like most of his fellows, to have looked upon it as a mere piece of social drill; in fact, he became a ringleader in a sort of strike of the senior boys against the compulsory prayers held at the Lyceum. As one of the 'liberating influences' undergone at this juncture he reckoned Halévy and Offenbach's operetta *La Belle Hélène*, the brilliant persiflage of which undermined his faculty of veneration—something to which he was dangerously prone by reason of his uneasiness *vis-à-vis* all authority, being partly the defiance of ordinary rebellious adolescence, partly also that of the 'excluded', jealous proletarian such as, through his mother, he believed himself to be.

Theologically, a more specific and a more enduring influence emanated from Theodore Parker, the Unitarian divine from Massachusetts, whose loose, unauthoritarian doctrines, based on immediate intuitions of God, the moral law and personal immortality, enjoyed some vogue in Sweden after their translation in the early and middle 'sixties. During the summer of

1866, when August was employed in a holiday tutorship, he was invited to preach in the village church of
Ösmo and apparently tried out his powers in a cautious
presentation of some of Parker's ideas. It may be that
the ambition of a clerical career then regained possession
of him for a short time. However, on his arrival at Uppsala for the autumn term of 1867, he had finally given up
any idea of taking holy orders.

5

For all his fertility, his cerebral activity and his explosive
assertions of personality, there is something unusually
unplanned and will-less in Strindberg's life when it is
viewed in its broader outlines. With no particular talent
for improvisation, he always lived from hand to mouth,
never knowing either where he was going or really
where he wanted to go. If, for instance, he went up to
the university resolved not to read Theology, that is
about the most positive statement which can be made
of his plans at that time. He certainly meant to take a
degree but, in an undergraduate, that almost amounts
to a self-evident proposition. He knew neither theoreti-
cally what taking a degree involved, nor practically how
he could stay the course. Some private tuition during
the summer of 1867 had left him with a net balance in
cash of 80 kronor; a devoted servant packed up some
food and domestic utensils for him and insisted on his
borrowing 15 kronor more; his father gave him a hand-
ful of cigars and told him to fend for himself.

Such were his equipment and his projects, if they may
be dignified by such names, when he arrived at Uppsala
for the autumn term of 1867. There were no college
tutors to give him guidance; some help he could have

gained from the professors, but, to wait formally upon them, custom imposed the wearing of evening dress, and August Strindberg had none. Emerging from and returning to squalid lodgings, he drifted about with others as raw and green as himself, looking in occasionally on such lectures as he and his mates might happen to hear of. It is almost comical that his first letter to his father says nothing whatever about his studies. When the end of term came, his 95 kronor had long been used up, the first of his lifelong debts had been incurred, and he himself was no nearer a clear notion of what he meant to do, either at the university or after he had left it.

The obvious thing, the necessary thing in fact, was not to return after the Christmas vacation. The first of the many occupations to which Strindberg then betook himself, early in 1868, was schoolmastering—and in the lower forms of the horrible old Klaraskola at that, where he now had to ram in that elementary pabulum which had so sickened him ten years earlier. He suffered physical nausea, as well, from the stench of the congregated children. A flame of idealism for his calling, however, managed to flicker through the miasma, and he dreamt of himself as the patriarch of some idyllic country school, a vision never to be realised. After a few months he obtained his second release from the Klaraskola by accepting a tutorship first in the household of Professor Oscar Sandahls and then in that of the refined, enlightened and sympathetic Jewish physician, Dr Axel Lamm, the only older person from whom there is record that Strindberg ever received any guidance worth the name. Dr Lamm encouraged him to write, he interested him in natural science and he instilled in him the ambition to become a doctor like himself. However, though he had reason to think that he had made satisfactory progress, he was, as we should say, 'ploughed in his Chemistry for the 1st M.B.', when he presented himself for that examination at Uppsala in the spring of 1869, and promptly abandoned Medicine, though to Chemistry he was later to come back.

Besides talk about science in Dr Lamm's house, Strindberg had also listened to discussions about the drama and the stage at a higher level, presumably, than that on which his cousin, the actor, moved during the Sunday dinners in Nortullsgatan. In consequence, he then read Schiller, burst into a wild flame of enthusiasm over *The Robbers* and strode about the military parade ground of the capital mouthing out the speeches of its hero, Carl Moor. To turn actor became his ambition now, and the Royal Theatre of the capital, Kungliga Dramatiska Teatern,[1] was peremptorily requested to let him make his début as the magnanimous bandit. The play, however, did not happen to be in the repertoire at that time, and Strindberg had to be content to begin as a nobleman in Bjørnson's *Mary Stuart in Scotland*, a part of eleven words, after which he was directed to train in the School of Dramatic Art (Elevskola). Nothing much came of that; for at the performance of the pupils early in the autumn of 1869, no part was found sufficiently humble for him to spoil; he was allowed to hold the prompt book, and neither the rehearsal rooms of the Elevskola nor the boards of Dramatiska Teatern were encumbered by his person again.

[1] Commonly called 'Dramaten'.

6

Strindberg was now approaching the end of his twenty-first year. On attaining his majority in January 1870, he became entitled to a share in his mother's trifling estate, after a short grim tussle wrested it from his father and, fortified with this money and, no doubt, Dr Lamm's ideas about university education, returned into residence at Uppsala for the spring term of 1870.

It cannot truthfully be said that Uppsala was a particularly enlivening place for anyone, less so in the early 1870's, perhaps, than it had been in 1867. Strindberg formed the impression, which was probably correct, that when he first went up to the University, there still lingered among the students some last faint traces of the happy-go-lucky *vie de bohême* of the mid-century, which Gunnar Wennerberg had indicated in *Gluntarne*, some disinterested pursuit of knowledge and general culture: in literature, the not altogether unsuccessful labours of Dietrichson to engender a new poetry and a more catholic appreciation were a recent memory. The professors to be sure were, for the most part, a mediocre lot, plodding through their texts at a snail's pace, and their callow critic may not have been wrong when he averred that the real interests of some of them centred on the evening's card-playing, pipe-smoking and toddy. In 1870 the quality of the staff had scarcely improved, and Strindberg thought that the students had definitely become more philistine and brutish.

Certainly, during his second period of residence at Uppsala, Strindberg no more came under the influence of some revered mentor, academic or extra-academic, than he had done in the autumn term of 1867. Even the contact with Dr Lamm seems to have lapsed. But now Strindberg worked with a will and read widely. On 19 September 1871 he was 'approved' in Modern Linguistics (French, German, English and Italian), the first of the oral examinations or *tentamina* which would go to make up his qualification for the degree of 'candidate in Philosophy'. A little later, an essay on the Danish poet Œhlenschläger[1] was submitted to the Professor of Aesthetics, Nyblom, who caustically adjudged it more suitable for a ladies' magazine than for an academic dissertation. Strindberg went on to pass the *tentamina* in philology, astronomy and politics, but, on receiving lower marks than he thought he deserved, finally threw up the sponge in March 1872.

Finance again was probably the main cause of his withdrawal. After his mother's legacy had given out, two school friends, Gustaf Eisen and Georg Törnquist, helped to support him, and for a short while he received an exhibition from King Charles himself; but the royal purse had to suffer a general retrenchment after the first instalment of 200 kronor had been paid out, and no compensatory source of revenue could be tapped.

7

A notable feature of Strindberg's second residence at Uppsala which most markedly distinguishes it from his first term, three years back, was his strong bent towards literary creation. One of its manifestations was the foundation, a few weeks after his return, of a small

---

[1] It was entitled 'Hakon Jarl eller Idealism och Realism', i.e. 'Earl Hakon, or, Idealism and Realism', and is printed in the second autobiographical volume, *The Time of Ferment*.

literary club by Axel Jäderin, Joseph Josephson and himself. In accordance with the fashion of the time, each member adopted a sobriquet, that which Strindberg chose being Frö—the name of an ancient Teutonic deity, in all probability an alternative name for the rather better known Freyr, brother of Freyja.[1] For what distinguished this society was its preoccupation with the mythology, history and civilisation of Germanic antiquity. At the same time as they affirmed general Scandinavian solidarity by their admiration of Danish and Norwegian literature and by their interest in the common past of Viking raids and sagas, the members were particularly concerned to purify the Swedish language through the replacement of loan-words taken from non-Scandinavian languages by native words that had become obsolete or which they coined, by analogy, from the Icelandic and other Scandinavian languages. They even wished Old Icelandic to take the place of Latin as the 'classical' language taught in schools.

The new society disclosed its characteristic bias by the name it took—'Runa'.[2] To 'Runa's' especial interests Strindberg's play *The Outlaw* (*Den Fredlöse*) and the fragment of *The Saga of Ån Bogsveig* (*Ån Bogsveigs Saga*), which he contributed to the club's almanack, *Vitter Kalender*, at Christmas 1872, bear witness.[3] Apart from himself and the literary historian Karl Warburg none of the members of 'Runa' left much of a mark on Swedish literature, and Strindberg soon became disgusted with them and with what they stood for. Writing

[1] 'Pacem voluptatemque largiens mortalibus', says the clerical chronicler Adam of Bremen, 'cujus etiam simulacrum fingunt ingenti priapo.'

[2] *Runa* = rune, the old Germanic character. In a letter Strindberg interpreted the word as meaning 'song' (*August Strindbergs Brev*, I, 25).

[3] *The Saga of Ån Bogsveig*, still in its fragmentary form, was reprinted in Strindberg's miscellany *I Vårbrytningen* (1881).

in 1875 to Fahlstedt, he thus characterised their former associates:

Jäderin:	Spiritually dead.
Wikström:	Cracked.
Fahlstedt:	[a blank, 'present company being excepted'].
Linck:	Fool.
Larsson:	Hypocrite.
Lundgren:	Sunk in brutish poverty.
Nilsson:	Dead.
Josephson:	Nothing.
Warburg:	Jew.
Victorin:	Thief.

8

The mention of *The Outlaw* and *The Saga of An Bogsveig* naturally leads to a consideration of Strindberg's literary beginnings in general. There is no direct evidence that Strindberg revealed a precocious bent to literature but some fairly strong evidence *e silentio* to the contrary. As was then expected almost as a natural product of grammar-school boys and undergraduates, he certainly obliged with an occasional copy of verses for a birthday or name-day or wedding party; that was all, however. Only one early poem has so far been traced in print: its title is 'The Visit' ('Besöket') and its date 1868, but it only appeared in an almanack for 1885, *Dagsländan*.[1]

The first really strong impetus to writing came to him by way of reaction to his failure as an actor. According to his own account, he sat down the very day after this fiasco and, within a few weeks, before the end of 1869, he had turned out no less than three plays. The first, a

[1] It does not, I think, occur in any later collection.

comedy in two acts, was soon torn up. We know no more about it than that it was called *A Name-Day Present* (*En Namnsdagsgåva*), that its matter was taken from *The Army Surgeon's Tales* (*Fältskärns Berättelser*, by the contemporary Finnish novelist Topelius), and that it obliquely showed a son's becoming reconciled with his stepmother through his father's intermediacy.

It was followed immediately by a prose drama in three acts, which worked out another of Strindberg's own problems: for *The Freethinker* (*Fritänkaren*) tells how a young village schoolmaster, whose acceptance of Parker's version of Christianity is fully set out in the first act, for the sake of that creed loses his fiancée, his employment and the confidence of his family. It failed to reach the boards, but was published in 1870 under the pseudonym of Härved Ulf. The review in the Stockholm *Aftonbladet* was severe; otherwise it passed virtually unnoticed.

The third play of 1869, *Hellas in Decline* (*Det sjunkande Hellas*), was rejected by the Royal Theatre; then, expanded into a five-act tragedy in blank verse (which Strindberg found he could compose very easily), it was renamed *Hermione* and sent in for one of the public competitions of the Swedish Academy of Literature: it did not win a prize, in fact was placed in the lowest category but one, but the official commendation of 'good isolated pictures together with a lively conception of the historical conditions'[1] was the only recognition which its author ever received from that august institution.

The author of *The Freethinker* then planned to develop the historical bases of his religious views by a grandiose drama on Jesus of Nazareth, which was never worked

[1] *Svenska Akademiens Handlingar*, XLVI (Stockholm, 1871), p. 17.

out. A play on King Eric XIV of Sweden[1] was, how
ever, carried to its conclusion in 1870, to suffer at once
the same fate as *A Name-Day Present*.

After this series of disappointments and failures,
Strindberg's friend Eisen very sensibly suggested to him
that he should write a play deliberately designed to gain
acceptance at the Royal Theatre: to this end he accordingly wrote, in rhymed verse, a one-act piece, *In Rome*
(*I Rom*), with relatively few characters, about the sculptor Thorvaldsen's early struggles. Not only received by
'Runa' with awestruck enthusiasm, the piece also
achieved its practical purpose. *In Rome* was acted eleven
times at Dramaten[2] and paved the way also for the acceptance and production of *The Outlaw* (*Den Fredlöse*),[3]
another one-act play, this time in unrhymed verse, laid in
medieval Iceland. It was the impression left by *The Outlaw* that induced King Charles to send for Strindberg and
award him the short-lived exhibition mentioned above.
Otherwise these two plays passed virtually unnoticed.

A heavier disappointment was caused by Strindberg's
inability to interest either a publisher or a theatrical
manager in the first drama of his which he rightly looked
upon as something more than a literary exercise. *Master
Olof* (*Mäster Olof*), which took for its hero the Swedish
religious reformer Olaus Petri, had been planned at
Uppsala in the autumn of 1871 and had been worked
out as a prose play of five acts between 8 June and
8 August 1872 on the island of Kymmendö in the
Stockholm *skärgård*. After its rejection by the Royal

[1] Not to be confused with the play on the same subject which he
published twenty-nine years later.   [2] September to November 1870.
[3] It was the reconstruction of a full-length tragedy, *Blotsven*, which
Strindberg wrote and destroyed in the autumn of 1870. *The Outlaw* was
finished early in 1871, acted at the Royal Theatre 16 October 1871
and published, first in the magazine *Nu* in 1876, then in Strindberg's
miscellany, *I Vårbrytningen* (1881).

Theatre, it was repeatedly rewritten, at last in a radically altered version, largely in the verse considered at that time virtually indispensable for historical drama. But that was not accepted for production either. Version B, the verse version, was published in 1878, the first, prose version, as part of the miscellany *At the Coming of Spring* (*I Vårbrytningen*) in 1881.

9

One may pause at this point in Strindberg's biography, at the age of twenty-three, when he was about to go into the world—and in the happy words of an American translator was no more than 'The Juvenile Poet and Revolter'—in order briefly to consider his equipment and the state of his mind and body.

He had grown into a handsome, well-grown young man, an excellent talker in a small circle and, when he chose to be so, a most charming companion. His eye glittered ominously and his hair rippled, but his face, as Georg Brandes thought,[1] was that of two men—one with the brow of the Jupiter of Orticoli, the other with the vulgar nose and chin of a Stockholm gutter-snipe. The anxieties about his future and the excessive cerebral activity of his last two years, to which rather too much drinking and wenching furnished no very satisfactory antidote, had further weakened a nervous system that had never been over-sound. Periods of moody depression alternated with others of exaltation or furious altercation, and he was already visited by fears of insanity.[2]

[1] *Germanisch-Romanische Monatsschrift*, VI, p. 321.
[2] In view of certain phenomena in his life and writings it may not, I think, be quite irrelevant to note that he suffered from persistent, painful strangury (A. J. Upvall, *August Strindberg* (1920), p. 17, on the evidence of a medical man who knew Strindberg personally during the 1870's). Cf. also T. Eklund, *Tjänstekvinnans Son* (1948), pp. 425 f.

Strindberg had acquitted himself more or less satisfactorily as a secondary school boy, obtaining a good
grounding in languages, notably in Latin and French,
and showing aptitude for historical and scientific studies.
To the past literature of his own country he neither then
nor later devoted much attention. The only independent interest of much significance which he evinced at
this time was in religion, where he had finally adopted
the standpoint of Theodore Parker. He firmly maintained it, we have seen, until the early 'seventies, he did
not altogether abandon it during the following ten or
twelve years, and one might well argue that he returned
to Unitarianism for the last years of his life; but the
creed underwent vicissitudes and periods of eclipse.

At the time that Strindberg was living in the household
of Dr Lamm, his sister reports him as once more in a state
of religious crisis, attributable with some certainty to the
effect on him, as on so many Scandinavians of his age, of
Ibsen's *Brand* (published in 1866), which inculcated no
particular creed, but urged the necessity of adopting one
and of ruthlessly bending the will to its demands.

The phase of conscience-searching and stern ethical
resolve did not last long, though its traces are clearly to
be seen amidst religious colouring of rather different
sorts in *The Freethinker* and *Master Olof*, and perhaps also
in the enthusiasm for Icelandic starkness which ani-
mated 'Runa'. The decline in Strindberg's religious
temperature was partly effected by the writings of the
Danish critic, Georg Brandes, who disliked not only
Brand's slogan 'All or Nothing', but also the form which
its application had taken in Ibsen's work. Strindberg
certainly knew Brandes's early essays,[1] one of which,

---

[1] *Criticisms and Portraits*, he says, illuminated his darkness like a lightning
flash.

dealing mainly with Shakespeare's *Henry IV* as an ex
ample of non-classical dramatic art, exercised a strong
and lasting influence on him, and sent him to a study of
Shakespeare's works as well as to the eighteenth-century
German authors inspired by Shakespeare. Brandes, too,
impressed him with his doctrine of relativity, infected
him with his own contempt for the romantic tradition in
current literature and for German idealistic philosophy
and firmly fixed it in his mind that an author must also
be a propagandist. As regards the first of these concep-
tions, that the phenomena of the mind owe their origin
and even their validity to circumstances of time and
place, Brandes received a very powerful enforcement in
Henry Thomas Buckle, whose *History of Civilisation in
England* Strindberg eagerly absorbed in the Swedish
translation of 1871–2 and who for the time being laid his
religious scruples and questing to rest, even if as late as
1872 he was reading Kierkegaard and declaring him
'just the man for me'.

In politics a not dissimilar change overtook Strindberg's outlook. His last days at school coincided with
the constitutional reforms which turned Sweden from a
semi-medieval polity of Four Estates into a modern
limited monarchy with a responsible two-chamber
legislature, and (Strindberg stood, without very much
knowledge or interest in the matter, but with a violent
prejudice against aristocratic privilege, on the side
of the political reformers.) But after Dr Lamm had
opened his eyes to the reactionary consequences, in
the realm of the arts, of putting power into the hands
of the supposedly liberal agrarians, a study of Tocqueville and Prévost-Paradol led him further on the
anti-democratic path. His youthful generous impulses
were further damped by Hartmann's pessimistic *Philo-*

sophy of the Unconscious and by Hartmann's master, Schopenhauer.

As for *belles lettres*, we are not so well informed as we might wish. But by 1872, or only a very little later, Strindberg certainly had acquired a considerable knowledge of Shakespeare, Goethe, Schiller, Victor Hugo, George Sand, Eugène Sue, Ibsen, Bjørnson, Dickens and contemporary American humorists such as Petroleum V. Nasby, Mark Twain and Bret Harte. He was a quick, omnivorous, but unsystematic reader.

THE LIFE, 1872–1891

I

In November 1872 Strindberg made, at Gothenburg, a second début as an actor: the experiment was as disastrous as the first and even shorter. Apart from that, Strindberg's breadwinning activities during the two and a half years that followed on his departure from Uppsala were concentrated on journalism. Earlier on, Dr Axel Lamm had suggested to him that they might collaborate in writing for the newspapers. The Stockholm *Aftonbladet* for 21 and 25 May 1869 printed an article entitled 'A Few Words about the Ethical Value of a Theatre for the Community', consisting of two parts, viz. a translation of Schiller's essay 'The Theatre considered as a Moral Institution', and an introduction touching on the Swedish peasant parties' hostility towards State theatres. According to the bibliographical expert Torsten Eklund,[2] the latter part was the work of Dr Lamm, the former that of his young friend. On 3 September 1869, the same newspaper printed a plea for 'The Right of Women to practise Medicine'; it was

[1] The chief authorities for this period, beside the general works noted at the head of Chapter I, are: Eklund, T., 'Strindbergs Verksamhet som Publicist 1869–1880' (in *Samlaren*, N.S., x (1930), 142); Jacobsen, H., *Strindberg och hans första Hustru* (1946, first published in Danish); Lundegård, A., *Några Strindbergsminnen* (1920); Mörner, B., *Den Strindberg jag känt* (1924); Smirnoff, Karin, *Strindbergs första Hustru* (2nd edition, 1926). The period of time covered is the same as in the second, third and fourth volumes of *The Son of the Bondwoman* and *A Madman's Defence*.

[2] In *Samlaren*, N.S., x (1930), 114. The Swedish titles of Strindberg's firstings are 'Några Ord om en Teaters moraliska Värde för ett Samhälle' and 'Om Qvinnans Berättigande att utöfva Läkaryrket'.

24

provoked by an editorial note in *The Lancet* for 7 August 1869[1] and, according to Strindberg himself, had been so radically revised by the editor as to say the exact opposite to what he intended.

Whether these two were the sole pieces of journalism which Strindberg produced at this time cannot be determined. But it is certain that he set himself seriously to the occupation only when it had virtually become a matter of life and death to him. From 1872 to 1880, especially during the first five years, he wrote very copiously for the newspapers and magazines: on the theatre (for *Stockholms Aftonpost*, *Dagens Nyheter*, *Najaden* and *Svalan*), on art exhibitions, on parliamentary debates—which were justly complained of, because, as the writer naïvely confessed, they represented what the speakers should have said rather than what they did say!—and on odd bits of history. There were a few articles on educational matters and rather more, but not very many, on books. In 1876, as S-g or Sg, he contributed a series of news-letters from the capital to *Göteborgs Handelstidning*; occasionally he had a sketch of a more imaginative sort printed, the earliest being a 'Letter from Sandhamn' ('Brev från Sandhamn', later called 'Sandhamn Storm') in *Dagens Nyheter* on 3 December 1873.

To his incisive, ironic style Strindberg owed such success as his journalism gained him, rather than to any expert knowledge, and he cannot be said to have become a force in the Swedish newspaper world. He wrote indiscriminately for newspapers and periodicals of every sort and political colour; very few of his articles he thought worth while reprinting later, and the two regular positions which he held were not exactly glorious: a

[1] 'Women and the Medical Profession', p. 206.

sub-editorship of *Svenska Medborgaren*, which mainly involved cutting up and sticking together news-items from the provincial press, and, for five months in 1873, the editorship of *Svensk Försäkringstidning*, a struggling organ of the insurance world, of which he probably wrote almost the whole of its ten issues. A magazine of his own, *Gazetten*, which he set up in 1876, did not survive its first number.

If, by his journalism, Strindberg was enabled to keep body and soul together, it was only by the narrowest of margins, and he must have soon realised that he could scarcely hope to gain a decent livelihood, let alone fame or influence, by its means. For a time he had thoughts of becoming a telegraphist and (in 1873) began his training at Sandhamn. A brighter outlook opened before him when, towards the end of 1874, he received an appointment as supernumerary assistant in the Royal Library. The pay, indeed, was small and had still to be eked out with newspaper articles, translations[1] and teaching; but the cataloguing work on which he was chiefly engaged proved light and congenial, and he enjoyed a relatively settled and honourable position with the title of Royal Secretary, 'Kunglig Sektern'.

2

In May 1875, then aged twenty-six, Strindberg for the first time met a woman with whom he fell violently and lastingly in love. Before this he had, as a schoolboy, been through the customary stage of adoring little girls and women a great deal older than himself, and after-

[1] Among these translations one may name some of Hans Christian Andersen's fairy-tales which were included in C. J. Bäckström's Swedish collection, *Sagor och Berättelser* (1877); cf. Blanck, A., in *Samlaren*, N.S., I (1920), 167.

wards he had indulged—perhaps not quite so frequently as sometimes he liked to make out—in the disgusting orgies with loose women which formed part and parcel of Swedish student life. After leaving Uppsala in 1872 he had entered into at least one liaison of a rather more serious nature, but none of these affairs, whatever effect they may have had on his health, seems to have stirred his imagination or left a specific trace on his imaginative writing.

The woman to whom he owed the revelation of passion and all its accompaniment of ecstasy and anguish was Sigrid (or Siri) von Essen,[1] the daughter of a Swedish-Finnish landed proprietor and, at that time, the wife of Baron Carl Gustaf Wrangel, a Captain in the Swedish Guards. Strindberg was soon on close personal terms with husband and wife. Realising the violence of his feelings and the fact that they were reciprocated, but, unwilling to fit himself into a *ménage à trois*, to which the easy-living Baron might not have been averse, Strindberg struggled to break away and took ship for Paris in the early autumn of that year (1875). Despair at parting from the loved one proved too strong for his resolution; he had himself dropped with the pilot and then did what he could to incur a fatal attack of pneumonia: but in vain. He returned to Stockholm. The Wrangels' marriage was dissolved in the following spring, and on 31 December 1877 Strindberg and Siri von Essen were married, less than two months before the birth of their first child, who was promptly put out to nurse, died within two days and was buried in the absence of both parents.

Siri von Essen, who was a year younger than Strindberg, loved him with an ardour answering to his own,

[1] Sigrid Sofia Matilda Elizabet von Essen was born at Jackarby Gård, near Borgå, Finland, in 1850 and died at Helsingfors in 1912.

and, all things considered, was to show uncommon devotion to him. But there was an ominous element in their relationship from the start. Siri was an extremely ambitious woman, not only on behalf of her husband, to whom she felt all the more attracted as the coming genius of his country's literature, but also for herself. Not designed by temperament to rest content with the part of a wife and mother, she craved a career of her own, a career on the stage,[1] for which, unfortunately, apart from a pretty and distinguished appearance, she seems to have had no great aptitude. Undeterred by the unlucky accident of her and Wrangel's only child's death a few days before, she made her *début* at the Royal Theatre on 27 January 1877 and, after a probationary period, was given a four-year contract there, lasting until 1882.

Siri's ideal of marriage was a partnership of two artists untrammelled by children and the like, in which she and her mate should form the centre of a brilliant Bohemian coterie. Strindberg acquiesced and, for a time, played his part loyally, doing what lay in his power towards his wife's professional advancement by coaching her and by writing plays with parts suitable for her to act. But it went against the grain: his wife's ideal of married life was never really his: he wanted more peace for reading and writing than her noisy friends and irregular hours allowed, he yearned for a more constant devotion, for the home comforts of the ordinary middle-class marriage which (at this time at least) made small appeal to his wife. It could hardly be avoided that in the course of time he should leave her a good deal to her own devices, and she had not sufficient moral ballast to resist the

[1] It would have been impossible for her to appear on the professional stage as the wife of an officer in the Guards.

temptations to which she was exposed. She seems to
have become intemperate, and Strindberg believed that
she succumbed to other vices as well.

Nevertheless, the first five years of their married life
were years of great, though not unalloyed, happiness.
The joint purse might be slender—in fact, in 1879,
Strindberg had to compound with his creditors—but,
first in Humlegårdsgatan, then in Östermalmsgatan, in
Stockholm, and during the summers on Kymmendö,
August and Siri lived comfortably, on easy terms with a
stimulating society of young actors, authors, journalists
and artists who looked up to them. Two little girls were
born to them, Karin in 1880 and Greta in 1881.[1] Siri
Strindberg had attained her ambition, even if the roles
of smart society ladies for which she was cast did not
completely satisfy it. Her husband had his secure place
in the bureaucracy and found a ready market in newspapers and magazines for the trifles it never took him
much trouble to throw off; he too was in a fair way to
realising his wife's ambition for himself, to becoming the
outstanding Swedish writer of his generation.

3

During the eight years in which he held his appointment
at the Royal Library (1874–82), Strindberg laid the
foundations of his literary fame. To be sure, the work
from which he had hoped so much, *Master Olof* (*Mäster
Olof*), did not help him much at first. Eventually, however, on 30 December 1881 the older, prose version was
produced at Nya Teatern in the capital, to be given no
less than forty-seven times. Meanwhile, Strindberg not

[1] Karin Strindberg married Vladimir Smirnoff in 1911; Greta Strindberg, who had become an actress and married her cousin Henry von Philp,
was killed in the railway accident in 1912.

only had completed and published three more dramas, *The Secret of the Guild* (*Gillets Hemlighet*, 1880) with a medieval setting, the trifling five-act comedy *In the Year '48* (*Anno Fyrtioåtta*, 1881) and the fairy-story play *Lucky Peter's Journey* (*Lycko-Pers Resa*, 1882), but had also ventured with considerable éclat into other literary fields.

In 1877 appeared his sketches of student life *Town and Gown*,[1] the harsh notes in which contrasted sharply with the sentimental attitude conventionally adopted in treating similar themes. Two years later, Strindberg incorporated the impressions received in the coterie of artists and journalists with which he had associated on leaving the University, into the novel *The Red Room*[2] (*Röda Rummet*, 1879). Written in much the same spirit as *Town and Gown*, but with greater penetration and wider scope, it was at once recognised as a masterpiece of literary realism—by no means with general approbation; for the squalor, physical and moral, of the society delineated, as well as the cynical point of view from which it was seen, roused much indignation; yet it went into four editions in less than two years, and Strindberg at the age of thirty was clearly seen as a man very seriously to be reckoned with both by friend and foe.

His official work in the Royal Library brought to his notice unpublished documents concerning the past relations of Sweden with Asia; he learnt some Chinese and composed a paper 'The Relations of Sweden with China and the Tartar Countries', which was read in translation to the French Académie des Inscriptions et Belles

---

[1] *Från Fjärdingen och Svartbäcken*; Fjärdingen and Svartbäcken being two well-known localities in Uppsala.

[2] This was an actual apartment in Bern's restaurant, Stockholm; Strindberg pretended that he was writing about the 'sixties; actually, the *milieu* is that of the middle 'seventies.

Lettres in 1879. Split up into four, with the addition of a more general essay on China, it was included in *Studies in the History of Civilisation* (*Kulturhistoriska Studier*, 1881). Strindberg now took up in earnest the history of his own country which, with Buckle before him, he wished to see treated in a manner quite different from that of the standard work of Geijer, for whom 'the history of Sweden was the history of its kings'. In collaboration with Claes Lundin, he issued in nine parts during 1880, 1881 and 1882 the popularly written sketches *Old Stockholm* (*Gamla Stockholm*) and, unaided this time, in 1881 and 1882 the rather more ambitious *Swedish People on Holy Days and Working Days* (*Svenska Folket i Hälg och Söcken*), of which the more or less imaginary tales *Swedish Destinies and Adventures* (*Svenska Öden och Äventyr*, 1881 and 1882) were an off-shoot.

In a manner, *The New State* (*Det nya Riket*, 1882), dealing with the political and social scene since the reforms of 1866, was designed to bring the historical survey down to date. But in fact, from the epigraph from *The Pickwick Papers*—'You are a humbug, sir.... I will speak plainer, if you wish it. An imposter, sir'—it was a series of highly satirical sketches in which, with harsh sarcastic wit, the author raked not only the conditions amid which the new constitution of 1866 had come into being, but also all the aspects of contemporary public life—such as the commercial enterprise of the new capitalism, the moulding and falsification of public opinion, the recruiting of officers for the army, the State theatres, the Swedish Academy—on which it pleased him to fasten.

4

Strindberg knew what he was about in writing *The New State* and trembled as he sent it into the world. It was a political pamphlet written from the point of view of an utter radical who seemed unable to draw attention to anything but fraud and mediocrity, and it was received as such: that is to say, rapturously by a certain number of uninfluential hotheads, with sardonic amusement by those who read it for its wit and with indignant repudiation by organised public opinion. Not only the book, but the author also became the object of attacks ranging over the whole of his personality, his doctrines and his literary production.

These attacks he felt, as usual, very keenly. *Lucky Peter's Journey* had not yet found a producer; *Sir Bengt's Wife*[1] had failed; and, in spite of the heartening success of *Master Olof*, its author conceived a general disgust against the theatre, which was increased on the Royal Theatre's decision to dispense with his wife's services and her failure to obtain regular employment on any other stage. He resigned his post at the Royal Library, resolved to earn his and his family's livelihood by the exercise of his pen alone, and in September 1883 they all quitted Sweden.[2]

It was not the first time that Strindberg had been outside his native country, but his visits to Copenhagen in 1869 and (by way of Christiansand, Bergen and Le Havre) to Paris in 1876 had only been short holidays. Now a wandering life began which continued for six years. First the Strindbergs settled for the autumn in

---

[1] Produced at Nya Teatern, 25 November 1882.
[2] A few weeks after this his *Poems in Verse and Prose* (*Dikter på Vers och Prosa*) were published, and in 1884 *Somnambulistic Nights by Broad Daylight* (*Sömngångarnätter på vakna Dagar*), a collection of free verse.

the Hôtel Beau Séjour at Grez, near Fontainebleau. In January 1884 they left France for French Switzerland, spending most of the year on the banks of Lake Geneva, at Ouchy and at Chexbres, where their boy Hans was born.[1] They spent 1885 again in France, most of 1886 in German-speaking Switzerland and 1887 near Lindau on the German shores of Lake Constance. In the autumn of the latter year the whole family moved to Denmark.

5

The decisive event of these years, and perhaps of Strindberg's life, was the confiscation by the public prosecutor of his collection of modern short stories _Married_ (*Giftas*), when it appeared at Stockholm in the early autumn of 1884, and the prosecution of the author that ensued. The passage to which objection was taken was that in which Strindberg wrote of the 'impudent fraud practised with Högstedt's Piccardon at 65 öre the pottle and Lettström's maize wafers at 1 krona the pound, which the priests give out to be the flesh and blood of the popular agitator Jesus of Nazareth, who was executed over 1800 years ago'. At first, acting on the advice of certain Russian refugees with whom he was then consorting, Strindberg proposed to let the publishers of *Married*, Messrs Bonnier, bear the brunt of the indictment for 'blasphemy against God or mocking of God's words or sacrament'. But in the end, Karl Otto Bonnier travelled out to Geneva to confer with him personally and persuaded him to go back to Sweden with him. Public opinion there was in some commotion. Strindberg's arrival at Stockholm station was greeted with an ovation, and a special performance of *Lucky*

[1] Hans Strindberg died in 1917.

Peter's Journey was given in his honour at the New Theatre. He took his stand in the dock when the trial was opened on 21 October 1884. The verdict, pronounced on 17 November after the jury had deliberated for four hours and a half, was 'Not Guilty'.

Strindberg, it was agreed, conducted his case with skill and dignity and, when the decision of the court was known, became the object of another popular demonstration.[1] He might feel, as never before in his life, that he had a strong and enthusiastic body of opinion behind him and could now, with his unequalled literary powers and his readiness to use them for furthering political and social ideas, make himself a redoubtable force in Swedish public life. But the excitement and tension of the whole affair had shaken him to the core of his being. 'My shot went off,' he declared, 'but it was too much for the gun. The pitcher has sprung.'

6

To establish the fact of Strindberg's nervous over-excitability (to put the condition at its lowest) one need scarcely go further than the two abortive attempts which, as a young man, he made to do away with himself on failing as an actor, first at Stockholm, then at Gothenburg. He was himself quite aware of it, he took medical advice and even—though unsuccessfully—petitioned to be admitted as a voluntary patient at a lunatic asylum at Uppsala.

For all that the early years of his association with Siri von Essen were the happiest and most settled in Strindberg's life, they had been years of stress too. From the

[1] The reports and comments of the newspapers are collected in *Svenska Pressen om A. Strindberg* (edited by H. S. 1885).

age of twenty-one, at any rate, Strindberg had been con-
sistently over-working. The total amount of his literary
output was very considerable, and it must be remembered that most of it had to be done in the hours left free
by the library, the snipping and pasting of the news-
paper-office and the lessons he was still obliged to give.
His relaxations were scarcely calculated to build up nervous strength, and there were very many occasions for
superficial jars in his abnormally erotic married life.
Karl Jaspers, a professor of philosophy who combines
insight into the psychology of artistic creation with a
medical training, holds[1] that definite schizophrenic symptoms were already apparent in him by 1882. When, in
the mood that has been described, Strindberg cut himself off from the irksome environment of Sweden, the
main cause of his distress did not automatically fall
away. It was not a case of *solvitur ambulando*. Now
that he and his wife had become completely dependent
on his pen, that is to say on the uncertainties of public
favour, his economic anxieties rather increased than
diminished, and the wandering, uprooted kind of life on
which he had embarked, with no prospect of an end to
it, revolted him. His constant ideal was that of the quiet
home, with wife and children in harmony about him,
and peace to mature his ideas and give them literary
shape—though, of course, this tranquillity could be
pleasantly tempered by little excursions, periods of complete solitude and stimulating interludes of other kinds.

It was thus on a mind already overwrought that the
shock of the prosecution and trial impinged. Karl Otto
Bonnier gives a picture of his companion dissolved in

[1] *Strindberg und Van Gogh* (1922), p. 55. Certain objections to Jasper's
findings, on the score of their insufficiency rather than of their inaccuracy,
are made by Martin Lamm in *Strindbergs Dramer*, II, 16n.

tears on a railway platform during their journey from Geneva to Stockholm. The dread of solitary confinement haunted him; it would, he believed, lead to the lunatic asylum as far as he himself was concerned and to the poorhouse for his wife and children. Judicially acquitted and popularly acclaimed though he might be, he nevertheless realised once more what powerful enemies he had raised up against himself—it was freely said that the Queen herself had instigated the prosecution—and it was no very far step from this realisation to the conviction that a widely ramified conspiracy was at work to deprive him of his freedom, his livelihood and his sanity.

The kernel of this conspiracy he believed to be made up of a league of women antagonised by his derisive criticisms of Ibsen's *Doll's House*—a feminist manifesto in his view—and by the detestation which elsewhere in *Married* he had evinced for emancipated females. When, no doubt with the kindest intentions, the Countess Leijonhufvud Adlersparre, a leader in the women's world of Sweden,[1] wrote his wife a letter of sympathy and encouragement on the occasion of his trial, not only were his suspicions of a concerted feminist action against him strengthened, but, much worse than that, he began to believe that his wife was being won over, had been won over, to the conspiracy. The enemy, he thought, had gained a footing in the inmost citadel of his private life.

It would be idle to assert that there was no foundation whatever for Strindberg's suspicions and for the mental anguish which they caused him. The anti-feminist attitude of *Married* had alienated a very considerable section

[1] She was mainly instrumental in founding the Frederika-Bremer-Förbundet in 1884 which had for its object to 'work for a healthy and steady development of the work of raising women's moral and intellectual as well as social and economic level'.

of advanced opinion and to that extent jeopardised his position as a radical leader—since to be 'advanced' and to be 'feminist' (in all their shades of meaning) were almost synonymous in Sweden in the early 1880's. After the confiscation of *Married* and a campaign against the alleged immorality of all 'Strindberg-Literature' which J. Personne launched three years later,[1] publishers too would be wary in accepting his manuscripts. Nor can there be any doubt either that, however loyal Siri might be as a wife and companion, she could not in all respects see eye to eye with her husband. The bohemian, wandering life they were leading might in itself not be so repugnant to her as it was to him—in fact, one of the less clearly formulated grievances he cherished against her was that she throve better than he in foreign *pensions* and amid casual acquaintances. On the other hand, she, an actress, was, in a foreign country, completely debarred from the exercise of her profession; and if any action—involving, no doubt, concessions of one sort or another—would have enabled her to resume something like the life she and Strindberg had led in the first years of their marriage, she could not but have applauded it. Above all, however, she was deeply concerned about her husband's mental state, which his latest manuscripts revealed, the growing frequency of his outbursts against women in general and her own friends in particular, and their mutual recriminations. It was not unnatural that she should—as privately she did—seek medical advice about him; and when this came to light, he leapt to the conclusion that she too wanted to have him certified insane and locked up.

[1] *Strindbergs-Litteraturen och Osedligheten bland Skolungdomen* (Stockholm, 1887); it urged the public prosecutor to take action under the provisions of the Swedish penal code against the dissemination of artistic matter offensive to decency and morality.

The effect of this state of things on his writing during the years immediately following the trial for blasphemy was, broadly speaking, two-fold. On the one hand Strindberg continued, first in short stories (the second collection of *Married*, 1886) and then in plays (like *The Comrades* and *The Father*), to launch his diatribes against emancipated and predatory women; and, at the same time, he subjected all his past life to careful scrutiny in order to account for the psychical and material misery into which he had lapsed. The outcome of the latter preoccupation was the series of autobiographical books, which, under the general title of *The Son of the Bondwoman* (*Tjänstekvinnans Son*) he began to write in 1886.

It is just possible that, obscurely, some cathartic intention underlay the characteristic work of these years—that Strindberg, realising the danger to his mental health, was trying by artistic means to rid himself of the poison of his suspicions and grievances. But, if that was so, the execution completely defeated its purpose: the more Strindberg absorbed himself in the iniquities of imaginary women and the supposed 'growth of his soul' (as the sub-title of *The Son of the Bondwoman* has it) the more real and justifiable his suspicions and his delusions came to appear to him.

7

It must not, however, be inferred that every page of *Married* and the autobiographies betrays Strindberg's morbid condition of mind, or that he was incapable of dwelling on anything but his grievances. There were whole chapters and essays and even one or two whole books composed in the middle 'eighties from which the subjective element was excluded and which testify to

Strindberg's readiness to receive external impressions and extend the range of his ideas. His output was extremely varied: nor does it betray any slackening of literary mastery.

On his return to Switzerland from Stockholm in the late autumn of 1884, he turned at once to setting down his recent experience, in 'The Confiscation Trip' ('Kvarstadsresan'),[1] to finishing off the tales which he grouped together as *Real Utopias* (*Utopier i Verkligheten*, published by Bonnier in 1885), and to the composition of the second, much more *outré* collection of short stories, *Married* (*Giftas II*), which appeared in the year after. Some of the latter, it may be mentioned, were originally written in French, of which Strindberg had acquired so good a command that, with rather more encouragement in the international market, he might well have become a predominantly French author. Immediately afterwards he wrote, also in French, *Contes et Fabliaux*, which did not appear until 1891 (in his own Swedish translation, *Fabler*).

The year 1886 was a year of immense activity. In about nine months he wrote the four volumes of his autobiography, the first and second of them, *The Son of the Bondwoman* (*Tjänstekvinnans Son*) and *The Time of Ferment* (*Jäsningstiden*) appearing in the late spring and early autumn respectively, while the publication of the third, *In the Red Room* (*I Röda Rummet*) was held over till the following year. The fourth part, *The Author* (*Författaren*), was refused by the publishers, who likewise declined to handle the love letters between Strindberg and his wife when he collected and prepared them for

---

[1] First printed in the periodical *Budkavlen* from 23 January to 17 April 1885; it is included in the collection *One Thing and Another* (*Likt och Olikt*) in vol. XVII of the Collected Works.

the press.[1] The comedy *Camp-Followers* (*Marodörer*) was written, but laid aside as unsatisfactory. This productiveness was diversified by an expedition to France during which Strindberg collected material for his book *Among French Peasants* (*Bland Franska Bönder*), published in 1889 and designed as the first instalment of a vast study of contemporary European peasantry in general.

The last-named, with its sympathetic treatment of *la crise agricole* of that time and of the manner in which the French rural population were tackling it, not only possesses some factual interest but illustrates also an interesting if short phase in the author's intellectual development. After Strindberg's propagandist zeal for Parkerism had been lulled by the relativity of Buckle and Brandes—the theory that creeds and religions could be explained by circumstances of time and place like other cultural phenomena—religious matters had ceased to interest him, and he had lapsed into a vague, rather indifferent acceptance of a non-dogmatic and non-sectarian deism. Such he publicly professed before his judges in 1884. The issue on which he had stood his trial forced him, however, to re-examine his religious position and drove him to the conclusion that fundamentally he had become an atheist. Casting about for some new faith he found it in something like the nature-worship and egalitarianism of Rousseau (whom he had already read at school and whom he now studied more thoroughly), with the corollaries that the true happiness of man depends on the immediacy of his contact with the soil and the equal distribution of wealth. He even accepted its political implications and, in subscribing to the theories

[1] They appeared as *He and She* (*Han och Hon*) as vol. XLV (1921) of the Collected Works. *The Author* was published in 1909. The last of the series is *Le Plaidoyer d'un Fou* (see pp. 42 and 47f. below).

of social democracy, abandoned his former isolated position of hostility both to aristocratic traditionalism and to liberalism. (The impetus which Rousseau's *Confessions* gave to his own autobiographical writing is also undeniable.)

It is true that he could not accept the new creed, to which Chernyshevsky, Lassalle, Henry George and the Saint-Simonians added their part, without some uneasiness. Like other revolutionaries, he read his Voltaire together with his Rousseau and was almost equally impressed. He could not forget that, admirable as an egalitarian peasant-community might be in many, perhaps the most important, respects, it was not very propitious to the graces and arts, and these he felt most unwilling to sacrifice.

In extremer moments, to be sure, he thought all art a luxury mankind could not afford; his main reason for differing from Tolstoy at this period lay, however, in the latter's utter repudiation of art. He was therefore ready to give ear to the new aestheticism of which his young Swedish friend, Verner von Heidenstam, was full when they were seeing one another almost daily.[1] Simultaneously, his anti-feminist animus led him to the conception that the 'war of the sexes', like socialistic agitation, was one of slaves versus masters, 'natural' slaves versus 'natural' masters. Living on German soil, impressed by the success of Bismarck's régime and the prestige of the officer-caste, he speedily abandoned Rousseauism for a form of Nietzscheism[2] *avant la lettre*. The daily application

---

[1] They travelled together in Italy and France in 1885, and Heidenstam was living in the castle of Brunegg while the Strindbergs were at Othmarsingen in Switzerland in 1886.

[2] Strindberg corresponded with Nietzsche and had a high opinion of him. But he never read *Zarathustra*, apparently, and probably knew little of his writing at first hand. His conception of Nietzsche's doctrines seems to have been the vulgar one: the right of the bully, or, at least, the superior

of hot tongs made him bearded like the paid; he had his photograph taken bending a rapier between his hands. By the time that it was published, the bucolic socialism of *Among French Peasants* had become obsolete to him, *ein überwundener Standpunkt.*

In Bavaria, in 1887, Strindberg wrote his second novel, *The People of Hemsö (Hemsöborna)*, a story of the Swedish archipelago, in which his older and newer creeds are found in such a state of artistically satisfying equilibrium that its author could later claim it as a pure piece of *l'art pour l'art*, completely exempt from all 'tendency'. There, as a more than Sophoclean rebuttal of the charge that he was out of his mind, which he believed his own wife was prepared to support, he also began, in French, the last of the autobiographical books, *Le Plaidoyer d'un Fou (A Madman's Defence)*,[1] and there too he finished *The Father (Fadren, 1887)*, the first of his naturalistic plays of modern life to see the light.[2]

8

On hearing that *The Father* was to be acted in Copenhagen,[3] Strindberg uprooted his family from Bavaria in November 1887 and went with them to Denmark. His

person, who for preference should be 'Nordic', to domineer over the weak, and a hatred of the religious and social sanctions which stood in the way of this.

[1] It seems that, when he had completed it, even Strindberg though it unfit for publication, at any rate for the time being. A bad German translation, *Die Beichte eines Thoren*, appeared without his consent in 1893, and the French original in 1895. The Swedish translation in the Collected Writings is by J. Lindquist and E. Staaf.

[2] *The Comrades (Kamraterna)* had been written earlier (1886), in the version *Camp-Followers (Marodörer)*, which, with the collaboration of Axel Lundegård, was revised in the late autumn of 1887. It was not published till the year after *The Father*.

[3] It was actually first presented at the Casino Theatre there, in Lundegård's Danish translation, on 14 November 1887.

general state was nearly desperate. Even the immense productiveness of the years in Switzerland and Germany had proved insufficient to defray the expenses of himself, his wife, his three children and their maid, modestly as they lived, and the small fund raised for their support by the publishers Bonnier and other well-wishers in 1886 had come to an end. His mental constitution had equally deteriorated (so that one of his very first errands in Denmark was to consult Dr Pontoppidan of the lunatic asylum at Roskilde). Distrust of his wife's loyalty to him, of her sexual morality and suitability to have charge of their children, had become ineradicable: he ceaselessly suborned his friends to spy upon her, he wanted to hypnotise her, so as to wrest the secrets of her infidelities from her, and at last he laid violent hands on her; the proposal of a divorce was now seriously entertained by both husband and wife. Fru Strindberg accompanied her husband on the northward journey, but when they stayed in the same hotel he insisted even on her taking her meals at a different table from his. On a newly made friend's asking him who the lady might be who had just passed them, he replied: 'She was once my wife, now she is my mistress.'

There was a short, last lifting of the clouds when it was thought that they might jointly run a theatre in Copenhagen to serve the whole of Scandinavia after the model of Antoine's new Théâtre Libre in Paris: Siri Strindberg, with her theatrical experience, was to act as manager and play the chief female parts, and of course some of the plays her husband had written and others which he was writing or projecting at this time, such as *Lady Julia* (*Fröken Julie*, 1888), *Creditors* (*Fordringsägare*, 1889) and *The Stronger* (*Den Starkare*, 1889), would be included in the repertoire. But 'Strindberg's Experimental

Theatre', inaugurated at the Dagmar Theatre on 9 March 1889, with a triple bill consisting of *The Stronger, Creditors* and *Lady Julia*, came to an abrupt end after three performances at Copenhagen and one at Malmö in Sweden, and the Danish impresario, Hunderup, who had produced *The Father* and had seemed disposed to venture on other plays by Strindberg, failed.

All this time (the autumn of 1887, most of 1888 and the beginning of 1889) Strindberg was living a wretched life in a deserted seaside villa by the Sound or in the former royal hunting lodge at Skovlyst—now abject, now proclaiming the rights of the superman—writing *A Madman's Defence*, his plays, *Tschandala*,[1] the short stories of *The Life of the Men of the Skerries* (*Skärkarlsliv*, published in 1888), adapting *The People of Hemsö* for the stage,[2] and desperately trying to raise the wind with one device after another. He thought of turning waiter or taking a course in business correspondence. To cap all, he went in terror of a criminal prosecution for an offence against a girl under the age of consent.[3]

In the summer of 1889, Strindberg was back in Sweden, living by himself in Stockholm, the archipelago and elsewhere and busy on his novel *In the Outer Skerries* (*I Havsbandet*, 1890), which has the same setting as *The People of Hemsö* and *The Life of the Men of the Skerries*, as well as on a few more naturalistic one-act plays[4] and similar trifles of no great importance.[5] Finally, in January

[1] This tale, intermediate in length between a novel and a short story, appeared first in Peter Nansen's Danish translation in 1889, then in the original Swedish in 1897.

[2] It was produced in Stockholm (as *Hemsöborna*) on 29 March 1889.

[3] Owing to a small misunderstanding about the relevant dates, Strindberg's fears were found to be groundless.

[4] *Pariah* (*Paria*) and *Simoom* (*Samum*) printed in the first part of the miscellany *Printed and Unprinted* (*Tryckt och Otryckt*, 1890).

[5] A further series of *Swedish Destinies and Adventures* appeared in 1891.

1891, the District Court of Värmdö (Häradsrätten i Värmdö Tingslag) heard his petition for divorce and, though he was unable to substantiate the most serious charges which he brought against his wife, the marriage was legally dissolved; Siri, however, was awarded custody of their children.

THE LIFE, 1891–1897

I

STRINDBERG declared that if his marriage with Siri von Essen had not been dissolved, either he would have murdered her, or she would have been the death of him. Yet the severance of the tie brought him no notable relief, chiefly perhaps because he had lost his children, who accompanied their mother to Finland.[2] Worse than this was the temporary decline in his artistic fertility. For about six years nothing of length, nothing of importance, came from his pen. Such sterility of course gravely impaired his economic position, which his divorce had scarcely made more promising, in view of his legal obligation to provide for the three children. Strindberg continued his vagabond life, travelling over the whole of Sweden, except Lapland, indigent and hopeless, so depressed that he could not even indulge himself in a first-class quarrel.

The only ray of light during the year following his divorce came from France, in the offer (which he declined) of the distinction of Officer in the Legion of Honour, called forth by his treatise *Les Relations de la*

[1] The chief authorities for this period, besides the general works listed at the beginning of Chapter I are: Hansson, O., 'Erinnerungen an August Strindberg', in *Neue Rundschau*, II (1912), 1536, 1724; Lamm, M., *Strindberg och Makterna* (1936); Paul, A., *Min Strindbergsbok* (2nd edition, 1930); Schleich, C. L., *Erinnerungen an Strindberg* (1917); Strindberg (formerly Uhl), Frida, *Lieb, Leid und Zeit* (1936, translated into English as *Marriage with Genius*, 1937). Strindberg told the story of his second marriage *modo suo* in the 'Quarantine Officer's Second Story' of *Fagervik and Skamsund* (*Fagervik och Skamsund*, 1902).

[2] Very naturally they took their mother's part, but later a rapprochement was effected: Karin, it seems, was married from his house.

France avec la Suède jusqu'à nos jours (1891). His imaginative powers in abeyance, Strindberg had recourse to his scholarly interests and also to the study of natural science—a pre-occupation to which we shall shortly return.

Strindberg's plight became widely known. As his family was kept from want by the generosity of one of the women whom he had denounced for the corruption of his wife, so he himself accepted the munificence of his friend Birger Mörner. In 1892 a fund of some Mks 1,500 was raised for his support by an appeal in the German periodical, *Die Zukunft*, and by its means he was enabled to cut himself free from Sweden and to travel to Germany. For some weeks beginning in October 1892 he lived quite near to the chief organisers of this charity, Ola Hansson and his wife 'Laura Marholm', at Friedrichshagen in the suburbs of Berlin. Ola Hansson was a Swedish man of letters, and 'Laura Marholm', a native of Riga who wrote in German, held a fairly conspicuous position in the higher journalism of her day. Both were active in making Scandinavian literature better known in Germany and introduced this eminent exponent to their circle of acquaintance in Friedrichshagen, made up mainly of the infusoria of naturalism, the brothers Heinrich and Julius Hart, Wilhelm Bölsche, Max Halbe, Bruno Wille and the like.[1] The Hanssons' propagandist efforts in his behoof did not prove outstandingly successful: to be sure, *Creditors* was produced at the Residenz-Theater in Berlin on 22 January 1893 and its seventy performances brought in some welcome royalties, he had the mixed gratification of seeing *A Madman's Defence* in a pirated German translation,

[1] In the winter of 1892–3 Strindberg also met the promoters of realistic drama in the German theatre, Paul Schlenther and Otto Brahm.

47

which led to scandal and an unsuccessful prosecution, and a few trifles were more legitimately printed in book-form or periodicals; but the days of his great fame in Germany still lay some years ahead.

Strindberg quickly found life in Friedrichshagen intolerable—'Friedrichs-Hell', he called it. He suspected Laura Marholm not merely of being a white-washed negress but also a 'Mrs Bluebeard'[1] who had marked him down as one of her victims. One morning he took French leave of his benefactors, sent a porter for his luggage and, before the end of 1892, was settled in Berlin. A favoured haunt of German artists and writers, as well as of their Scandinavian *confrères*, was Türck's tavern at the corner of Unter den Linden and the Neue Wilhelmstrasse, to which Strindberg gave the sobriquet 'Zum Schwarzen Ferkel', 'The Black Porker'. The most eminent of its frequenters were the German authors Richard Dehmel and Otto Hartleben, the Finnish composer Sibelius, the Norwegian artists Edvard Munch and Christian Krohg (who were both to paint Strindberg), the Swedish man of science Bengt Lidforss, the Polish writer Stanislas Przbyszevsky (to whom Strindberg refers as Popoffsky),[2] the Danish poet Holger Drachmann, Ibsen's German translator Julius Elias, the Swedish-Finnish novelist Tavastjerna and his wife, the Norwegian authors Gunnar Heiberg and Knut Hamsun, as well as Dr Schleich and Adolf Paul, who later published their recollections of Strindberg. Strindberg used, somewhat unmelodiously, to play the guitar and

[1] 'Fru Blåskägg'.
[2] The chapter on Strindberg in Herman, M., *Un Sataniste Polonais, Stanislas Przybyszewski* (Paris, 1939), p. 150, is of little account, but there is some interesting matter (184 et passim) about Przybyszevsky's later wife Dagny Juel, who appears to have been one of Strindberg's mistresses in the spring of 1893.

sing to them. He consumed great quantities of spirits, never, however, appearing to be the worse for them. Women were not excluded, and the evenings frequently ended in an orgy.

2

A few weeks after moving into Berlin, in January 1893, Strindberg met Frida Uhl, the daughter of the Austrian critic and novelist Friedrich von Uhl, editor of the official *Wiener Zeitung*. She herself, then aged twenty, was beginning to earn her living as a journalist in Berlin and soon came to gravitate to 'The Black Porker'. In many respects—rather younger, rather less refined, rather less attractive, but equally self-willed and emancipated—she resembled what Siri von Essen had been eighteen years earlier. In spite of that, Strindberg not merely fell in love, as he was doing right and left at this time, but even determined to make her his second wife; nor did the young lady, apparently, find much reluctance in herself to overcome.

The recent cession of Heligoland from Great Britain to the German Empire had left behind some anomalies in the Registrar-General's department, which made that North Sea island a favourite resort of continental couples with reasons for marrying in haste and secrecy. Strindberg and Frida Uhl made the stormy passage thither at the end of April 1893, answered the local clergyman's searching questions to his satisfaction and were duly married according to the rites of the Church of England on 2 May.

If Strindberg had cherished hopes of settling down to a quiet life of domesticity and literary productiveness with his second wife, they proved completely vain. A short honeymoon was spent in Heligoland, at Gravesend and in London, to the heat and fog of which the newly married pair had been lured by chimerical expectations of what Justin McCarthy by his criticisms, William Heinemann the publisher and J. T. Grein with his Independent Theatre would do to provide Strindberg with a warm personal welcome and a large, remunerative public. But before June was out, leaving his wife behind, he crossed the North Sea again. During the next few months, his traces, now solitary, now accompanied by those of Frida, are to be found at Hamburg, in the island of Rügen, at Ardagger and Dornach, on the Danube in Nether Austria (where his wife's grandparents lived), in Berlin, by the Mondsee in Salzkammergut, at Brno in Moravia, at Versailles and in Paris.

At Dornach the birth of the only child of the marriage, Kierstin, took place in May 1894, but even this brought no stability. The word divorce had already been pronounced in serious intent between the spouses. Strindberg accused his wife of spying on him, restricting his independence and trying to 'manage' him as an author (like Laura Marholm) and also of compromising him by her free mode of life (like Siri); and in November 1894, at the Gare du Nord in Paris, they parted for the last time. Two months later Frida instituted divorce proceedings in Vienna. Kierstin was lost to him, like Siri's three children.

3

Shortly after the Stockholm trial in 1884, it has been said, Strindberg pronounced himself an atheist. For some time after this, his speculations all proceeded from a basis of monism and materialism: thought, ideas, religion, art were functions of the physical brain. Such was the frame of mind in which he wrote his short stories of married life, the five volumes of autobiography and the 'naturalist' dramas such as *The Father* and *Lady Julia*.

Already during this span of some five years, however, Strindberg, like many of his contemporaries, was taking a keen interest in what might be called the direct action of mind on mind, 'The Battle of the Brains', as he called it. By this he meant not merely the clash of wills in argument and in purposive action, the stuff of drama, but, in addition, the subtler power of suggestion, to be observed most unmistakably in the phenomena of hypnotism. The denouement in both *The Father* and *Lady Julia* is brought about, or at any rate furthered, by something like mesmeric means—the Captain being lulled by his old nurse into meekly putting on the lunatic's strait-jacket, Lady Julia going off to cut her throat as her paramour intends that she shall. Strindberg read about Charcot's experiments, attended hypnotic *séances* and appears himself to have possessed mesmeric powers. Frida Uhl reports two instances of this: when during the rough passage to Heligoland he put her into so deep a sleep that on arrival she could be carried, still unconscious, from the ship to their hotel; and when he persuaded her, at the time of Kierstin's birth, that parturition was a pleasurable process and—at least for a time—caused her pangs to cease.

To Strindberg, as to many others at this time who interested themselves in such phenomena, they appeared to be a violation of 'the laws of nature', as in his most rigid materialistic days he had conceived them. As was natural to a man of his temperament, the doctrines and findings of those whom he looked upon as the accredited exponents of the 'laws of nature', the professional scientists, at once became suspect, and he cast about for more immediately demonstrable loopholes in their system through which he might discredit them.

During the period of his creative impotence in the early and middle 'nineties, he was constantly engaged in scientific studies. In ten years' time he expected to be a member of the Swedish Academy of Science and a professor, as well as the possessor of six foreign orders of knighthood.[1] At first it was Botany[2] that absorbed him —even if, as Birger Mörner reports, he would go on his botanical expeditions in Skåne wearing the high silk hat in which he afterwards sat indoors, noting the results. From Botany he turned to Chemistry[3] and Optics. Wherever he went he set up some sort of cramped and primitive laboratory, even on a hotel wash-stand if necessary: when Frida parted from him he carefully unpacked his 'six crucibles of fine porcelain, a pair of tongs and a packet of pure sulphur'. His friend Schleich, a man of science himself, describes him as a painstaking and accurate experimenter,[4] but, on the other hand, there is rather a Chekhovian touch in his

[1] *Från Fjärdingen till Blå Tornet*, p. 218.

[2] 'Det Svensk Natur' (Swedish Nature), first printed in the almanack *Svea* for 1896, 'Skånska Landskap' (The Landscape of Skåne), which appeared together in the fourth volume of *Tryckt och Otryckt* (1896), and *Jardin des Plantes* (in Swedish, Göteborg, 1896) are Strindberg's most substantial botanical studies. 'Det Svensk Natur' was intended as the first part of a large-scale description of the whole of Sweden, in its physical aspect, which Strindberg planned in 1889.

[3] Strindberg's chemical investigations and theories are contained in *Antibarbarus*, first published in Bengt Lidforss's German translation (1894) and then in the original Swedish in 1906, and in various contributions (in French) to the Paris periodicals *L'Initiation* and *L'Hyperchémie* during 1896, 1897 and 1898. *Sylva Sylvarum* (in French, Paris, 1896) is made up of some of these contributions and of *Jardin des Plantes*. The scientific writings of this time are collected in vol. XVII of *Samlade Skrifter*.

[4] Cf. Bengt Lidforss, 'Strindberg som Naturforskare', in *Fragment och Miniatyrer* (3rd ed., 1923).

disdaining on one occasion to commit suicide with cyanide of potassium because he feared that the home-made compound would not work! In 1895 he wrote to a friend that he was engaged on

Colour Photography.
The Telescope.
Atmospheric electricity as a motive power.
Iodine from coal.
Phosphorus from sulphur.
Sulphuric acid from alum-slate.
Nickel plating without nickel.
Discoveries in the metallurgy of iron and steel.[1]

The general subject which, it will be seen, chiefly interested him at that moment was the transmutation of elements. He had come to believe that the atomic scale of modern chemistry was a fraudulent invention foisted on the world by 'the learned camorra' of professors, that in fact the number of basic elements in the physical world was much smaller than that which they proclaimed and that the medieval scientists were, in this respect,[2] nearer the truth than their present-day successors. The chemical manufacture of gold from baser metals was an undertaking that naturally made the greatest appeal to one with his craving for power and his crippling poverty; and to that he applied himself for long periods. From being a chemist he became an alchemist, nor did he disdain the appellation.

By two avenues, therefore, hypnotism and alchemy, Strindberg approached the fashionable occultism of his

---

[1] Mörner, *Den Strindberg jag känt* (1924), p. 120.
[2] And, indeed, in others. Strindberg believed that the sun revolved round the earth.

day.[1] He believed in reincarnation and cherished the hope that the spirit of Edgar Allan Poe, who died in the year that he was born, had passed into his body.[2] He accepted Sar Peladan as a true mage.[3] It was inevitable that he should thereby be brought into touch with theosophy, and, though I do not suppose that Strindberg ever fully accepted a sufficient number of their cardinal principles to be ranked among the theosophists himself, he certainly went with them so far as to abandon completely his monistic materialism. He claimed that he only adopted a belief in a spirit world, distinct from, but interpenetrating the world of physical phenomena, as a 'working hypothesis', and, for all his superstition, there is a case for saying[4] that he never completely abandoned his scepticism. He wished to believe, but he never plunged headlong into belief, constantly trying to find his bearings, however thick the fog about him might be, and noting as regularly and meticulously as he could all the observations that would help him to orientate himself.[5] For long spans of time, nevertheless, the 'working hypothesis' became an all-embracing principle to him, an article of faith; and up to the time of his death he never jettisoned it altogether.

This mental process, it must constantly be borne in mind, took place in a personality reduced to despair by

[1] 'My role', he wrote in a letter of 3 March 1896 (Lamm, *Strindberg och Makterna*, p. 89) 'seems to be to provide the link between science on the one side and occultism and religion on the other.'

[2] The theory is invalidated by the fact that Poe died ten months after Strindberg's birth.

[3] As well as the incarnation of the Nietzschean superman.

[4] Jaspers, K., *Strindberg und Van Gogh* (1922), p. 62.

[5] *Inferno* and *Legends* were compiled from diaries which he kept and sometimes quoted (e.g. *Samlade Skrifter*, xxviii, 68 ff.). Strindberg continued to post an (unpublished) 'occult diary' until 1908, and several entries of the kind with which this diary was presumably filled are to be found also in the later 'Blue Books'.

poverty and material anxiety, weakened by absinthe, racked with a sense of guilt through his failure as a son, husband and father, convinced of a conspiracy against himself by all those who had suffered injury and insult from him either in his personal relations or in his writings, and haunted by the ever-present dread not only of direct assault, but also of incarceration as a debtor, criminal, anarchist, lunatic or the mere victim of private animosity. The legal proceedings taken against the pirated German translation of *A Madman's Defence* brought back all the terrors of the trial at Stockholm nine years earlier. At times, all self-control and sense of reality were lost. He experienced, he said, exactly what Swedenborg had defined as 'Devastatio'.

The culmination of the process goes by the name of the 'Inferno Crisis', from the book *Inferno*, in which (and *Legender*, *Legends*) he described the dreadful months when he came nearest to losing his reason for good.

4

As Jaspers says,[1] it is difficult, invidious and not very helpful to attach labels to Strindberg's mental state at the time of the 'Inferno Crisis' or even to the experiences which he reported. It has, for instance, been doubted[2] whether he could in a technical sense be said to have suffered from visual and oral hallucinations, but what is ordinarily meant by the term seems clearly to have befallen him when, for instance, he heard three Scandinavian women playing the piano simultaneously in the next house with the intent of driving him crazy, and

[1] Jaspers, K., *Strindberg und Van Gogh* (1922), p. 55.
[2] E.g. by Hedén, p. 244. A. J. Upvall, on the other hand, maintains that 'during his stay at Gravesend he became subject to real visual hallucinations' (*August Strindberg, a Psychoanalytic Study*, p. 73).

when he encountered a divine figure during his walks in Paris.

The most striking element in this internal turmoil has yet to be mentioned. It was Strindberg's conviction, encouraged and confirmed by the study of Swedenborg, to whom he came by way of Balzac's *Séraphita*, that his mental torment was primarily instigated by a positive outside agency, designated by him as 'the Powers' (*Makterna*). What exactly they were he never finally determined. Indeed, as is sufficiently remarkable, he rarely appears to have speculated in general terms about their nature: their impingement upon himself was all that concerned him.[1] Now, when he identified Hell and the world in which he moved and had his being, the Powers seemed to him autonomous forces of evil, now they were conceived as the agents of human adversaries who had acquired magical control over them, now they were instruments of God.[2] At one moment he blindly submitted himself to their dictates, turned up at random a page in the Bible, and guided his actions by the first text to meet his eye; at another, he could note quite seriously: 'The servant has made the most wretched coffee imaginable. I offer it as a sacrifice to the Powers and from this day on I take chocolate, without murmuring.' But an unseen force was at work, of that he

[1] In the belief, however, that all suffering, inflicted by the Powers, must be retribution for past malfeasance, he declared once that Dreyfus, having obviously suffered, must therefore have been guilty (Lamm, M., *Strindberg och Makterna*, p. 140). In another place (*Inferno*, p. 195) he throws out the suggestion that the purpose of the Powers is to produce the Nietzschean superman.

[2] Lamm notes (*Strindberg och Makterna*, 1936, p. 71) that in a letter to Hedlund of January 1896 Strindberg, for the first time in his middle years, expressed his belief in a personal God and in immortality. He also (p. 95) acutely remarks on the progressive change in the name which Strindberg gives to the Powers: they are successively called 'les invisibles', 'les puissances', 'les puissances inconnues', 'les puissances invisibles' and 'les puissances de l'invisible'.

had no doubt, sometimes contenting itself with putting messages of warning in his way—as when he saw a couple of twigs taking the shape of the letters P and Y, to put him on his guard against 'Popoffsky'—but more generally interpreted as one chastening him for past misdeeds, urging him to contrition and demanding reconciliation.

At this spiritual crisis Strindberg often bethought himself of the conventional consolations of religion and purposed to avail himself of them. But, as his scepticism never completely left him, neither did his radical non-conformity. It is characteristic that on the occasion of his encounter with the divine apparition near the Luxembourg Gardens he should immediately begin an argument about feminism—whereupon the figure vanished. The Bible, Swedenborg and *The Imitation of Christ* might be his constant reading, churches and communities might beckon him, but he could not bow his stiff neck to make himself completely a theosophist—Helena Blavatsky was a woman!—or a Swedenborgian or a Protestant or a Roman Catholic. The hatred of Christianity which Nietzsche had instilled in him was hard to eradicate. More than once he planned to enter a monastery and on one occasion he actually did take up his residence in one. The phrase fairly accurately describes the proceeding. When it came to the actual point Strindberg looked upon the refuge of a monastery as something like the Hotel Orfila in Paris, a place with a calm, pious, benign atmosphere, from which women were excluded, but where he himself could freely come and go and where he could give himself up without interruptions to his researches and his writing. Repeatedly he reverted to a monastic ideal in his writing, but the monastery of his dreams had very little to do with religion—let alone with any fixed creed: it was really a residential club, for men only.[1] The concrete experiment which he made in August 1898, at the Benedictine abbey of Maredsous in Belgium, appears to have been given up after only twenty-four hours.

5

The sketch just given of Strindberg in the throes of his 'Inferno Crisis' is of course the outcome of a double schematism, that effected by himself in the records which he composed for publication[2] and that made by the critic mainly on the basis of the author's own earlier scheme. In reality the crisis could not but be vastly more complex and more discontinuous. Strindberg was always subject to uncommon vicissitudes of mood; what he thought and felt one day was not only (except in very rare instances) no logical corollary of what he had thought the day before, but might even amount to the direct opposite.

In concluding the present chapter one may perhaps profitably do two things: first, give a brief chronicle of the main events in Strindberg's life during the three years following on his separation from his second wife, and secondly, quote some medical opinions on the nature of his mental malady.

[1] Strindberg draws up an elaborate programme for his ideal monastery in a letter to Leo Litmansson (*Från Fjärdingen till Blå Tornet*, pp. 259 ff.); he also handles the subject in his imaginative writing, notably in *Black Banners*.

[2] An instance of his suppressing what did not fit into the artistic scheme of *Inferno* is the visit of his sister Anna von Philp and her husband to Paris in the summer of 1896, with the quite cheerful, 'normal' parties which were then given to speed him on his return to Sweden (Philp, A. v. and Hartzell, N., *Strindbergs Systrar berätta*, 1926, p. 79). J. Mortensen (*Strindberg som jag minnes honom*, p. 21) also gives the damaging information that friends at Lund, knowing him to be short of matter, freely invented tales of the supernatural which he included in *Legender*.

When Frida Uhl and Strindberg parted in November 1894, he was more deeply immersed in his alchemy than ever before. The prime reason for his breaking away from the relative tranquillity of Dornach and travelling to Paris that autumn had been that he might be near the Parisian alchemists, who responded to his advances by appointing him a professor in their College (without, it seems, either duties or stipend). With such zeal did he cast himself upon his retorts and crucibles after bidding Frida his last farewell that he very seriously damaged his hands and had to enter the hospital of St Louis in Paris for treatment early in the New Year, 1895.

It was about this time that Strindberg's persecution-mania and the accumulation of horrors in its train mounted to their first great climax, and it is here that the account given in *Inferno* begins. The spring and summer of that year, 1895, however saw him restored in good measure to physical and mental health; he worked happily at his experiments and at articles for *Le Figaro*, *Gil Blas*, *La Science Française*, *La Revue des Revues* and *Le Temps*. He was acquiring a considerable if eccentric reputation in Paris, as a mage, a painter and the author of *Lady Julia*, *Creditors* and *The Father*, which were performed in French translations in 1893 and 1894.

During the autumn of 1895 the second and most devastating phase of the great crisis overtook him and lasted until the summer of 1896. Then Strindberg uprooted himself from demon-rid Paris and went to South Sweden, to Lund and to Ystad, where he submitted himself to medical treatment by Dr Eliasson, as he had already done during a flying visit the summer before. It was not long before he persuaded himself that Dr Eliasson was intending to do away with him, and he fled from Ystad. But the treatment—in which cold water figured prominently[1]—had done him good and he was further pacified by a stay of some weeks with his little daughter Kierstin and her mother's grandparents at Dornach. The latter were practising Roman Catholics; their example and the study of Swedenborg which he now seriously undertook gave his speculations and dreams a more specifically religious turn than they had had before.

Inferno, which describes Strindberg's state from November 1894 to November 1896, was apparently sketched out at Ystad and Dornach; it was completed at Lund, where Strindberg came to rest in December 1896 and where he also wrote *Legends*, the continuation and supplement of the account given in *Inferno*.[2] The life of the little university town and intercourse with a few intelligent, level-headed and sympathetic friends often bored him, but acted as the sedative which he most needed. The worst of his crisis was definitely behind him, though it was not quite overpassed. He continued his occultist-scientific researches and still gave way from time to time to his morbid *wanderlust*. He was in Paris again for the autumn and winter of 1897–8 and, once more, for a short while in the summer of 1898, but no longer haunted and hunted by the dreadful Powers. The Erinyes had become the Eumenides. In the autumn of 1897 he took up, after an interval of some seven years, his imaginative writing again.[3]

[1] Uddgren, G., *Boken om Strindberg* (1912), p. 173.

[2] *Inferno* and most of *Legends* were originally written in French; the first (Swedish) editions are of 1897 and 1898 respectively. The original of *Inferno* was published at Paris in 1898.

[3] I have stretched a point in excluding *Inferno* and *Legends* from this category. Since 1890 there had only been the fairy play, *The Keys of Heaven* (*Himmelrikets Nycklar*, published in April 1892, immediately after completion) and six equally insignificant one-act plays published in 1893.

6

For the medical aspect of Strindberg's mental condition I will cite four authorities whose professional training and profound interest in the case eminently qualify them to speak.

The first is Dr Schleich, who not only knew Strindberg intimately, but also was one of the few people with whom he never quarrelled; he did not, however, see or (as far as is known) correspond with him during the years of supreme crisis, from 1894 to 1897. He says:

> One should not believe that Strindberg was ever insane. He was always clear, logical, certain in his judgement [*denksicher*] and paid regard to all objections with the greatest equanimity. Perhaps he was somewhat prone to notions of persecution, but they never had anything hallucinatory [*zwanghaftes*] about them, being always, where I could check them, the result of all too well grounded distrust.[1]

Jaspers deliberately dissents from this judgment and goes on to the following pronouncement:

> To decide in general terms whether Strindberg was mentally deranged is valueless [*nichtssagend*]; for if, proceeding from a predetermined definition, one assumes mental derangement only when the individual loses his self-possession, his bearings and power to arrange his ideas, then Strindberg was not mentally deranged. But he suffered from a well-known, characterisable process which occupied more than twenty years of his life and which one can call schizophrene, paraphrene or paranoia—the words do not matter.
>
> In Strindberg is to be found an abundance of psychological, incomprehensible, heterogeneous, but recognisably co-ordinated symptoms (recurring in similar cases in similar sequences or arrangement)....The process begins in the 1880's. It advances in two great waves [*Schüben*] which reach their crest in 1887 and 1896.[2]

[1] Schleich, C. L., *Erinnerungen an Strindberg* (1917).
[2] Jaspers, K., *Strindberg und Van Gogh* (1922), p. 55.

Rahmer says of the beginning of the 'Inferno Crisis':

We have here a first and fundamental clinical symptom of incipient psychosis: depression, sadness, ill-humour; and the further symptoms of the psychic diathesis: love of solitude, a shy or hostile attitude towards the outer world. Add to that psychic anesthesia, and, in connection therewith, indifference towards all personal relationships, even the most important.

He then goes on to assert that it is clear to the layman

that we have to do with a morbid condition and serious psychosis, which has developed gradually and slowly, reached its climax amid violent manifestations of lunacy and delusions and then slowly diminished under suitable treatment.

Rahmer concludes that the condition is not paranoia (since the victim regards the persecution to which he is subjected as cruel, but not undeserved); he thinks it a 'typical classic case of melancholia, manifesting itself at the climax of its development as *melancholia demono-maniaca*'.[1]

Upvall, who calls his book a psychoanalytic study, after concurring with the diagnosis of W. Hirsch[2] that Strindberg's malady was *paranoia simplex chronica*, assumes 'with some degree of certainty that Strindberg was homosexual'[3] and reaches the general conclusion that 'we are dealing with a real case of psycho-sexual fixation on the mother, with its consequent concomitant feature—hatred of the father'.[4]

[1] Rahmer, S., *August Strindberg, eine pathologische Studie* (1907), pp. 9, 25, 26.
[2] In *Genius and Degeneration*, which I have not seen.
[3] For an overt manifestation of which there seems no evidence whatever.
[4] Upvall, A. J., *August Strindberg* (Boston, 1920), pp. 33, 68.

THE LIFE, 1897–1912

I

THE Strindberg who took up quarters with his friend, the editor Waldemar Bülow, at Lund late in 1896 was a very different person from the reveller in the Black Porker's sty of less than four years before. The purgatory—or hell, as he thought it—that had seared his soul had left its brand also on the outer man. He was not yet forty-eight years of age, but those who saw him casually about the streets and public resorts of Lund and knew little or nothing about him took him for a harmless eccentric, definitely beyond the prime of life, even old. This is how my colleague's father, Johan Mortensen, then a youngish graduate of the university, describes his first sight of him:

> One day in the middle of December 1896 I was sitting at one o'clock lunching with a few friends in the restaurant of the Lund town-hall....Suddenly the door opened, and gently and noiselessly there glided into the room a person who instantly arrested my attention. The man was August Strindberg....
>
> Even if I had not known who he was, his dress and appearance would have attracted my notice. He was clad in sporting costume, not so common then as now, at any rate in a dining-room: with yellow shoes, check stockings,

---

[1] For the matter of this chapter, besides the general works listed at the head of Chapter I, the following should be consulted: Falck, A., *Fem År med Strindberg* (1935); Falkner, F., *August Strindberg i Blå Tornet* (1921); Lidforss, B., *A. Strindberg och den litterära Nittiotalsreklamen* (1910); Mortensen, J., *Strindberg som jag minnes honom* (1931); Uddgren, G., *Andra Boken om Strindberg* (1912; English translation, as *Strindberg the Man*, Boston, Mass., 1920). Strindberg's letters to Harriet Bosse, with valuable notes by her, are published as *Strindberg till Harriet Bosse* (1932).

knickerbockers and a jacket fastened by a belt. The colour of the suit resembled the plumage of a sparrow-hawk, that is to say, it was black-grey with white dots. You have only to substitute a pair of boots for the yellow shoes and you have him precisely as in the photograph he had taken of himself in Switzerland, when he was full of Russian nihilism and imitated Tolstoy as closely as possible.

More peculiar, however, even than his costume was the look of the man. Once you had seen his face, you could not forget it, it was so striking. His hair, rich, brushed up, black —even if already sprinkled with silver threads—fell in soft, moist locks round his head and over his enormous, beautifully shaped forehead, which dominated his whole face. It was like the mountain in a landscape. Everything sunny and dark was reflected on those heights.... The big, light-grey eyes with their black iris, almost like a horse's, looked round timidly and with an expression of dejection. Weary, sorrowful eyes, as if washed in tears.

Everything moreover in Strindberg's manner testified to his shyness. His tread was noiseless, and with downcast eyes he took a seat at the table which stood nearest the door, turning his back on the company which had been sitting in the room before him. After he had, in an inaudible voice, ordered something of the waiter who had bustled up to him, he provided his plate with something from the common side-board, had some soup ladled out to him and, after this enterprising performance, withdrew timidly to his table.[1]

Strindberg, as was ever afterwards to remain his custom,[2] worked hard at his writing-table for some hours in the morning, at about one o'clock took his lunch out, with a nap at home to follow, and, in the evening, liked

[1] Mortensen, J., *Strindberg som jag minnes honom* (1931), pp. 7 ff. With this may be compared a description of Strindberg's appearance four years earlier, the full horror of which is, perhaps, best appreciated in the American translation: 'Suit of a large-checkered material with large cuffs on the pantaloons, a short yellowish-gray topcoat, a loud necktie, a cane of exaggerated size and a well-polished silk hat which hardly could be induced to remain on Strindberg's fluffy lion's·mane' (Uddgren, G., *Strindberg the Man*, 1920, p. 60).

[2] In his latter days at Stockholm the routine was somewhat varied since Strindberg altered the time-table of his meals: he then worked from eight to four with a long break for *frukost* at 11.

to foregather for conversation with some friends and acquaintances, when a great deal of tobacco and not a little whisky and punch were consumed. These new associates were, for the most part, like Johan Mortensen, young graduates or senior students of the university, members of the advanced discussion club, 'The Young Veterans' (*De unga Gubbarna*), who received Strindberg in a friendly manner as an intellectual equal, but with no especial awe either for his literary eminence or for the personal sufferings which he had undergone. The time between lunch and dinner hung rather heavy, and Strindberg carried on, but with declining zeal, his scientific investigations. A photograph of the time shows him posed in front of an imposing array of chemical bottles in his private laboratory.

2

His literary work had again gained the upper hand. To begin with, *Inferno* and *Legends* were cast into their final form. Then, late in 1897, Strindberg took up his playwriting again, with *To Damascus* (*Till Damaskus*), the first two inseparable parts of which, completed by the summer of 1898, were published in the autumn of that year.[1] *Advent* and *There are Crimes and Crimes* (*Brott och Brott*) followed in swift succession and appeared in one volume entitled *Before a Higher Court* (*Vid högre Rätt*) during the spring of 1899.

The titles of two of these plays just mentioned point to a religious content, and all three are permeated by a religious spirit. Even if the Powers no longer seemed devilish to Strindberg, their function had been (and

---

[1] The third part, *Till Damaskus III*, was added to the other two in the edition of 1904.

might still be) to chasten him, to bring him, however imperfectly, to a state of humility and the recognition that 'There's a divinity that shapes our ends, Rough-hew them how we will.'[1] In his new writings Strindberg would, he resolved, set forth his new-found convictions, exhibit in imagined personages something akin to the process by which he had himself reached those conclusions and preach their acceptance to the public.

3

On 22 January 1899 Strindberg celebrated his fiftieth birthday at Lund almost as quietly as if he had been an Englishman. The great rising luminary of Swedish literature from fifteen and twenty years back had suffered eclipse during the years of his sterility between 1890 and 1897 and he was only just beginning to emerge from it again. The return to public notice is largely attributable to *Inferno*, *Legends* and *To Damascus*, but also to a most successful revival of the prose *Master Olof*, which had gone through fifty performances at Vasa Teatern in Stockholm during the season 1897–8. Henceforward the name Strindberg always remained well to the fore in the literary and theatrical world of Sweden, sometimes lauded, sometimes execrated.

The recent success of *Master Olof* on the stage greatly cheered him and, seconded by Johan Mortensen's specific encouragement, stimulated him to return to his old love, historical drama; so, having dispatched the manuscript of *There are Crimes and Crimes* to the publisher within five weeks of his birthday, he set himself to the first of a group of new plays which were all completed before

[1] He marked this passage with especial approval in his own copy of *Hamlet* (Bulman, J., *Strindberg and Shakespeare*, 1933, p. 108).

the end of 1899. A further specific stimulus was provided by Shakespeare's chronicle plays,[1] which (together with the tragedies) Strindberg knew well and continued to admire: he believed them to form, in conception and execution, one single series embracing all of English history that the author's audiences might wish to know; and he conceived the ambition to compose a vast dramatic history of his country, demonstrating how God's intentions towards the Swedish people had been made manifest.

The play which Strindberg began to write in February 1899, *The Saga of the Folkungs* (*Folkungasagan*, 1899),[2] took its subject from a chapter of medieval history, but, though he went out of his way to furnish links with *The Saga of the Folkungs*, both in *Gustav Vasa* and *Erik XIV* he leaped fairly into the sixteenth century, intending that these two plays should form a trilogy together with the older *Master Olof*.[3] Then, passing by a project of a play about Charles IX of Sweden, he made another jump, into the second quarter of the seventeenth century, with *Gustavus Adolphus* (*Gustav Adolf*).[4]

By the time that the four historical dramas of 1899 were completed, Strindberg had left Lund. He spent the summer of that year at Furusund, the 'Fagervik' of his book *Fagervik and Skamsund* (*Fagervik och Skamsund*, 1902), where he was at pains to meet again and, when necessary, make his peace with members of his family,

---

[1] It was reinforced by the reading of Starbäck-Bäckström's *Tales from Swedish History* (*Berättelser ur Svenska Historien*); Afzelius and Fryxell were already familiar to him.

[2] Produced at Svenska Teatern, Stockholm, on 25 January 1901 and given there twenty-three times in all.

[3] *Gustav Vasa* and *Erik XIV* were very successfully presented at Svenska Teatern, Stockholm, on 17 October 1899 and 30 November 1899 respectively. Both were published that year.

[4] Published 1900, first acted at the Circus, Stockholm, in 1912.

67

as well as other friends of bygone times. (He also resumed, about now, amicable relations with the children of his first marriage.) The holiday season ended, he took up his abode in Stockholm and there remained firmly rooted, apart from summer holidays (usually at Furusund),[1] until his death.

The reception given to *Gustav Vasa* and *Erik XIV* at Svenska Teatern induced the Royal Theatre, which had hitherto scarcely shown itself lavish in its support of Strindberg, to make overtures for the rights of *To Damascus*. The double play was eventually put on in the autumn of 1900; and soon afterwards the same house had two new pieces by Strindberg in the bill: *Easter* (*Påsk*), which in a story of modern life mirrored the moods appropriate to Maundy Thursday, Good Friday and Easter, and the rather meaningless, light trifle of the Punch-and-Judy variety, *Caspar's Shrove-Tuesday* (*Kaspers Fet-tisdag*), which were presented on 4 April 1901 and 16 April 1901 respectively.[2]

4

During a performance of Shakespeare's *Midsummer Night's Dream*[3] Strindberg, who was attending it with an eye to the casting of *To Damascus*, first saw a newcomer to Dramaten's personnel, an actress of Norwegian provenance called Harriet Bosse; with her performance of Puck she cast a spell on him. He recommended that to her be allotted the part of the Lady in *To Damascus*, and

[1] Strindberg was at Furusund in 1900, 1904 and 1905, at Hornbæk in 1901 and at Grisslehamn in 1903.

[2] *Easter* was very well received and was published in book form the same year; the other piece was only repeated once and did not appear in print until it was included in vol. XXXIII of the *Samlade Skrifter* in 1921.

[3] It is significant that, apart from the rude mechanicals, Strindberg disliked this play, because of its careful construction.

this she eventually played, to his great satisfaction—and not to his alone. Fröken Bosse was then twenty-two years old and Strindberg only a few weeks short of fifty-two. In spite of the serious disparity of age, a warm friendship quickly sprang up between Puck and the white-haired author, and by March 1901 Strindberg found himself in an advanced stage of courtship, carried on partly in letters of great tenderness and solemnity, but finally clinched by the affirmative answer to the question: 'Fröken Harriet Bosse, would you like to have a baby by me?' There was, however, a grave obstacle to the marriage. Frida Uhl's divorce had never been ratified. Strindberg proposed to flout the conventions with a kind of pragmatic sanction, a declaration affixed by himself to the church door announcing that he and Fröken Bosse were man and wife. His argument: 'My young, new-born undenominational faith is stronger than that of the half-infidel professional parson's, has greater power than the curate to call down the blessing of the Lord, God the Creator, upon our union'[1]—did not, however, impress the young lady and her mother. In the event, the difficulties remaining over the second divorce proved quickly surmountable, and in May 1901 Harriet Bosse and Strindberg were legally married.

Although it was not the most melodramatic of his three unhappy marriages, Strindberg's marriage with Harriet Bosse proved the most tragic. Both parties entered into it with a full knowledge of the great dangers they were braving. They commanded a deep fund of mutual love, admiration and understanding—which, in fact, was never wholly exhausted—a more continuous good will, both of an earthly and an almost religious kind, than ever had graced the relations of Strindberg

[1] Letter to Harriet Bosse of 16 April 1901.

with Siri von Essen or Frida Uhl. Both were conscious of playing for the highest stakes, putting down all their pride and determination to make a success of what presumably everybody else at once wrote off as inescapable disaster. Harriet Bosse, young and inexperienced as she was, felt—as perhaps Frida Uhl already had done—that she had taken upon herself a mission,[1] that of bringing back to a full life and full human contentment the man so cruelly maimed and desolated by his contacts with the world and with her own sex in particular. None knew better than Strindberg what that maiming and desolation had been, still were, and how horrible their intenser repetition would be; now had come to him the supreme opportunity of rising superior to his afflictions; if, with all the fund of good will and love, in material circumstances more propitious perhaps than they had ever been to him, his new great enterprise should fail, the fault would clearly be his and his alone: he would know that he was unfit to live with, unfit to live the life of which he and his young wife dreamed.

But in spite of all this, the marriage ended as the two other marriages had done. Within a month of the nuptials, serious disagreements between the parties had begun, and their effect was only postponed, not annulled by the birth of an idolised daughter, Anne-Marie, on 25 March 1902. Eighteen months later, wife and child left 40 Karlavägen[2] (where Strindberg and Harriet Bosse had lived since their marriage and where Strindberg was to continue to live alone till 1908), and the con-

[1] *Från Fjärdingen till Blå Tornet*, p. 336. Strindberg felt this too and, in fact, had wished it.
[2] On returning to Stockholm in the autumn of 1899, Strindberg had gone into furnished rooms at 5 Narvavägen, which he soon left for 31 Banérgatan. No. 40 Karlavägen (where he had Siri's first husband for a neighbour, a circumstance dimly mirrored in *The Storm*) has been renumbered and is now No. 80.

jugal separation was complete, though an affectionate friendship—on Strindberg's side, at least, a passionate friendship—was maintained until Harriet Bosse re-married and so quenched Strindberg's lingering, last hope of an ultimate reunion. The marriage was legally dissolved in November 1904.

It is a curious fact that, with his deep, instinctive longing for a life of quiet domesticity, with his ineradi-cable distrust of intelligent and emancipated women who would not be satisfied with playing the moon to a husband's sun, and with his practical knowledge of what it meant for him to co-habit with someone of this kind, Strindberg should, for the third time, have taken to wife a woman of very marked individuality and intelli-gence, with a profession of her own which she did not propose to abandon, and with a clear-sighted, most reso-lute will. This bride of a month, this girl of three-and-twenty, when her husband did not see fit to take her on the wedding trip they had planned together, packed up and went off on her honeymoon by herself![1] There seems to have been no defiance, at any time, on Harriet Bosse's part, but a calm determination to have what all reasonable beings would look upon as her proper rights.

It was on this twin rock of individuality that the ship foundered. What Strindberg wanted of a wife was what just this wife could not give him, without being someone other than herself. He loved her for being Puck about the house, he did not want to obliterate her individual-ity, but any suggestion to his suspicious mind that that individuality was making claims or asserting rights or exercising influence that in the remotest way seemed to infringe on his own individuality put him beside

[1] Strindberg of course soon joined her (at Hornbæk in Denmark).

71

himself.[1] Violent protests and recriminations could not but follow. Strindberg saw the rocks with the clear eyes of despair, he knew the frightfulness of the shipwreck. 'What was the quarrel about?' he wrote. 'Yes, that we should, both of us, preserve our personalities when they threatened to melt into one. You had the advantage, for you had friends—I was absolutely alone, a captive under the spell of yourself and the child.'

5

The year 1901 witnessed not only the happiness of Strindberg's courtship and wedding with Harriet Bosse, but equally the writing and publication of *The Dance of Death* (*Dödsdansen*),[2] one of his most powerful and idiosyncratic 'modern' plays—formally, it is a double play, a play in two parts—in which he gave the ghastliest expression to the war of extermination between the two sexes, as he conceived it. In much mellower mood, he then wrote three plays which have a strong family-resemblance and were published together in 1902: *The Crown Bride* (*Kronbruden*), *Swan-white* (*Svanevit*) and *The Dream Play* (*Drömspelet*). All of them clearly reveal the strong influence of Maeterlinck, both as dramatist and thinker; Strindberg made translations from *Le Trésor des Humbles* for his wife; he harboured the strong wish that she should play a principal part in each of these plays, especially in *Swan-white*, to which he constantly referred as 'our' *Swan-white*.

But the hope of this kind of partnership likewise came to nothing, and none of the 'Maeterlinckian' plays saw

[1] And there was the uncurbable, atavistic fear that in the life she led away from him his wife might compromise his 'honour'.

[2] The first part had its *première* at Intima Teatern, Stockholm, on 8 September 1909; the second at the same house on 1 October 1909.

the footlights until long after Strindberg and Harriet Bosse had parted.[1]

Nor had, all this time, Strindberg's interest in the historical drama slackened. After *Gustavus Adolphus* came, in 1901, *Engelbrekt* and *Charles XII* (*Carl XII*); in 1903, *Kristina* (with Gustavus Adolphus's famous daughter for heroine) and *Gustavus III* (*Gustav III*), which brings the Swedish story down to the very end of the eighteenth century.[2]

The Royal Theatre presented *Charles XII* (13 February 1902) and managed to keep it in the bill for sixteen performances; but the treatment of Sweden's great soldier-king as, almost, a somnambulist courting death amid the ruins of his career could arouse no enthusiasm and not much more interest. All the other plays of these years proved, for the time being at least, even less successful. Strindberg, it was felt, had over-written himself in a two-fold sense: ever since 1899 he had been throwing at the theatre-managers' heads a larger output than the conditions of the market could allow them to dispose of satisfactorily; and, at the same time, the rapidity of the execution raised suspicions of careless workmanship, which the habitually lax construction and flat characterisation of his longer plays confirmed.

Strindberg never again completely lost his hold on the Swedish public's attention, and in Germany, thanks to

---

[1] *The Dream Play* and *The Crown Bride* were first acted at Svenska Teatern on 17 April 1907 and 14 September 1907 respectively; *Swanwhite*, with Fanny Falkner in the title-part, proved one of the outstanding successes of Intima Teatern (see below), where it was presented on 30 October 1908 and given 150 times in all.

[2] *Engelbrekt*, produced at Svenska Teatern on 3 December 1901, was done three times; none of the others in this group for the time being. One historical play lying outside the group, *The Nightingale of Wittenberg* (*Näktergalen i Wittenberg*), written and published in 1904, was intended primarily for the German market, as a dramatic-biographical presentation of Martin Luther.

the untiring efforts of his translator Emil Schering, he was slowly gaining devotees and royalties. Yet the justifiably bright hopes of 1899 and 1900, it could not be gainsaid, had been disappointed. From early in 1904 for a matter of nearly four years Strindberg completely ceased writing for the theatre with which, he declared, he had conceived an utter disgust as mere 'pose, superficiality and calculation'.

6

Correspondingly, Strindberg was drawn back to narrative composition, first in the collection of largely autobiographical short stories, *Fagervik and Skamsund (Fagervik och Skamsund)*,[1] completed and published in the autumn of 1902, and then in *Fairy-Tales (Sagor,* 1903) and the lengthier prose-sketch, *Alone (Ensam,* 1903), which together with certain parts of *Word-Play and Minor Art (Ordalek och Småkonst,* 1905)[2] reflect the mood induced by his separation from his third wife. A little later, when (for the time being) he had completely renounced the drama, he attempted to infuse into a different medium the kind of inspiration which had lain at the back of his historical plays and with which he had sought to animate them. It was natural that the result should be a last collection of short stories from Swedish history, linking on to the series he had begun more than twenty years past, the *New Swedish Destinies (Nya Svenska Öden),* which show little novelty either in period or in treatment; but Strindberg now also extended his scope to other countries' history, with the even less successful *Historical Miniatures (Historiska Miniatyrer),* in which his notorious

---

[1] These are topographical proper names, such as might actually occur. The innuendo in them has been rendered in the published English translation *Fair Haven and Foul Strand*.

[2] This was an expansion of an item originally intended for (and included in) *Fagervik and Skamsund*.

deficiency in factual accuracy and in a genuine historical sense lacked the counterpoise which his sympathy for his own people in the circumstances of their past had given him.[1] In 1907 Strindberg published together two long 'short-stories', *The Roofing-Spree* and *The Scape-Goat* (*Taklagsöl, Syndabocken*).

The outstanding works during this period of his life, from 1903 to 1907, were the two closely related novels, *The Gothic Rooms* (*Götiska Rummen*) and *Black Banners* (*Svarta Fanor*), both completed in 1904. Strindberg's aim in them was to carry on the descriptions of Stockholm literary life begun with *The Red Room*, and a palpable concrete link lies to hand in two of the three titles, the actual premises, Berns Salong, on which *The Red Room* was focused, having in the course of time been redecorated to form a suite of 'Gothic rooms'. An obvious weakness in the undertaking lay in the circumstances that Strindberg, for a very definite purpose, projected to do for the 1890's 'mutatis mutandis' what *The Red Room* had done for the 1870's and that he was in a singularly poor position to write about the 1890's by reason of his four years' exile abroad, followed by a span of three years in Lund: even in 1890 and 1891 he had kept aloof from Stockholm[2] and had scant relations with authors, journalists and artists. It is not surprising that, becoming conscious of this defect, Strindberg should have to pad out both books, *The Gothic Rooms* especially, with matter irrelevant to his main subject.

[1] Both these collections were written in 1905, when the *Historical Miniatures* were published; the *New Swedish Destinies* appeared in the following year.

[2] It may be objected that in his confused campaign Strindberg was attacking phenomena of the 1880's quite as much as those of the 1890's— Geijerstam, for instance, was much more of a leader in the former than in the latter decade. Strindberg, however, was nearly as much out of touch with Sweden from 1883 (when the newer literature really started getting under way) to 1889 as he was in the ten years following.

The very definite purpose actuating Strindberg, to which allusion was made in the last paragraph, was to discredit the whole literary movement in Sweden contemporary with his own career, in spite of its extreme disparity and the fact that its variety mirrored much the same vicissitudes of aim, taste and method to which his own work was subjected. For fifteen years or so (1884–99) Strindberg had been a 'lost leader', and since his great 'come back' both to Stockholm and to the literary field had failed to win the recognition which, both on historical and on artistic grounds, he thought due to him. Swedish literature, even if he had opened a new era with *The Red Room*, had gone its own way regardless of him, and poets, dramatists and fiction-writers had gained reputations, sometimes great reputations, in the fields which Strindberg had himself cultivated and to which, in some instances, he had been the first in Sweden to point the way. Of this, however, there was little recognition, certainly not enough for Strindberg's sensitive *amour propre*. Gustav af Geijerstam, Heidenstam, Fröding[1]—even Selma Lagerlöf and other women— might be lauded as the great regenerators of Swedish prose and verse; yet not only was this aspect of Strindberg's work generally overlooked, but the critics whose duty it should have been to repair such omissions indulged themselves even in adverse reviews of his writing on literary and moral grounds![2] He meant to read all his rivals and adversaries a lesson: to exhibit the pro-

[1] Fröding, perhaps the greatest among Sweden's fine lyricists, Strindberg looked upon as a mere purveyor of smut, though he took an interest in his visions and hallucinations.

[2] Thus, in a general survey of literature contained in *Det Nya Sverige* (1908), the critic and literary historian Böök declared that drama represented the weakest spot in recent Swedish literature and picked out only a single play for commendation—Tor Hedberg's *Johan Ulfstjerna*; Strindberg's writings are scarcely more than curiosities.

gressive degeneration of the nation's cultural life, the greed, corruption and pitiful ideals of its intellectual leaders, their shameless log-rolling, their foolish, ignoble characters.

A novel might have carried out part of this programme pungently and effectively, yet without giving offence, but scarcely the whole of it, nor would it have been Strindberg's way, for all the spiritual regeneration which he was claiming for himself. As commonly happened with him—as most notoriously had happened at the time when he wrote his great autobiographical series —the more he let his imagination play upon his grievances, to cast them into literary shape, the more intolerable they came to appear to him and the more certainly he attributed them to direct personal enmity. *Black Banners*, therefore, and *The Gothic Rooms* too, although in a smaller degree, are outbursts of insensate, obscene fury against everything that Strindberg detested in the world which he thought he saw and, what is more, against representative individuals whom for the most part readers had no difficulty whatever in identifying. Those most copiously spattered with opprobrium were Hanna Paj (i.e. the great leader of the women's cause in Sweden, Ellen Key), Professor Stenkåhl (i.e. Professor Warburg, the literary pundit) and, especially, Zachris (i.e. Gustav af Geijerstam). Geijerstam and Strindberg had been close friends about twenty years before, but Strindberg's resentment against him had been steadily piling up, since Geijerstam had been of service to him first at the time of the Stockholm trial and later as literary director of Messrs Gernandt, the Stockholm publishing firm which handled most of Strindberg's work at the turn of the century; but he was, it must be confessed, a second-rate personage and a second-hand writer, who had not been above decking himself with Strindberg's own feathers, and it was galling to have advice proffered, even with the best of intentions, from such a one, who was sometimes held up, to boot, as the great literary pioneer of the 1880's.

The fictitious personages Hanna Paj, Stenkåhl and Zachris all appeared in *Black Banners*, and even Strindberg hesitated to loose this book upon the world. He held it back for three years. During this time his justifiable feelings of outrage and of neglect by literary Sweden steadily grew, probably in proportion as his pathetic hopes of eventual reconciliation with Harriet Bosse waned. In 1907 the Lord spoke, through the Book of Jonah, and the bomb burst, its effects intensified by Strindberg's issuing as a form of commentary on *Black Banners*, and by no means as a palinode, the first of his 'Blue Books'.[1] The personal reactions can be readily imagined. But the secondary consequence was a series of partisan surveys of the literary scene during the past quarter of a century which often (though not universally) issued in the conclusion that the undeniable advance of Swedish literature during the past quarter of a century had been made in spite of Strindberg and that in fact such degenerate phenomena as his last novels fastened on owed their origin to him. Strindberg's project of rehabilitating his literary name, at whatever cost to his reputation as a man, was only very partially realised.

---

[1] *En Blå Bok* appeared in 1907. It was followed in 1908 by *A New Blue Book* (*En Ny Blå Bok*) and *A Blue Book III* (*En Blå Bok den Tredje*) and in 1912 by *An Extra Blue Book* (*En Extra Blå Bok*). All are formless collections of essays, rarely more than a page in length, running through the whole gamut of the author's preoccupations, interests and literary hobbies at the time of composition.

7

Just at this time, at the height of the storm raised by *Black Banners*, Strindberg entered into partnership with the young actor-manager August Falck, who had been touring the provinces with *Lady Julia*[1] and *Pariah*. Falck was enterprising; he and Strindberg between them were able (not without difficulty) to raise some capital. By this conjunction, Strindberg found himself in a position to realise one of his longest and most dearly cherished ambitions, namely, to be actively concerned in the direction of a theatre. A tiny house, with room for only 161 persons, was secured on the Norra Bantorget in Stockholm, and on 26 November 1907 Intima Teatern opened with the first performance on any stage of Strindberg's play *The Pelican* (*Pelikanen*). It had been the promoters' intention to present a varied repertoire of plays by dramatists old and new, provided they were suitable to the slender material resources at their command: they dreamed of Euripides's *Hippolytus*, of Racine's *Phèdre*, of Wagner's *Tristan and Isolde* (without the music). In the event, however, they confined themselves to Strindberg, of whom in exactly three years they produced no less than twenty-four pieces (giving preference naturally to those which had never been acted before) with a grand total of 1147 performances. The greatest success was achieved by *Easter*, acted 182 times, the second greatest by *Swan-white*, acted 152 times.[2]

---

[1] His production of the piece at Lund on 18 September 1906 was the first in Sweden.

[2] Falck, A., *Fem År med Strindberg* (1935), gives a full table of performances (p. 358). The company sometimes divided, part of it giving performances in the provinces and abroad; the latter are not included in the figures given.

The latter was the only play that Strindberg produced in person, and his personal contact with Intima Teatern was never very close, in the sense that he did not haunt the building or represent the management in its contacts with the world outside. He did, however, concern himself actively with the *décor* of plays selected for production and made some useful written criticisms of what he observed at rehearsals; and he also published in 1908 and 1909 the five pamphlets of observations on the drama which were later collected to form volume L of his *Samlade Skrifter*.[1]

The knowledge of having at his command a theatre not only ready to perform his plays, but even crying out for additions to its repertoire, gave Strindberg the stimulus he needed to send him back again to writing drama. With Intima Teatern's limitations of personnel, acting space and material equipment in mind, he invented a special kind of drama which, standing in relation to ordinary drama as chamber music does to orchestral music, he designated Chamber-Plays (*Kammarspel*). The collection of *Kammarspel*, comprising *The Pelican*, *The Storm* (*Oväder*), *After the Fire* (*Brända Tomten*),[2] and *The Ghost Sonata* (*Spöksonaten*), was published at the end of 1907, all the constituent plays being performed at Intima Teatern by 22 January 1908.[3]

For production at his own theatre Strindberg also wrote a play which made heavier demands on it than

[1] Viz. *Memorandum* (1908), *Hamlet* (1908), *Julius Caesar* (1908), *Shakespeares Macbeth* (1909) and *Öppna Brev till Intima Teatern* (1909).

[2] The title really means 'The Burnt-Out Site', the incitement to the play having come from Strindberg's passing 14 Nortullsgatan one morning and finding that his old home there had been burnt down.

[3] A fifth Chamber-Play, *The Black Glove* (*Svarta Handsken*, 1909), was written somewhat later and never acted at Intima Teatern. It was first acted in the Swedish provinces and then presented under the title *Jul* (*Christmas*) at Nya Intima Teatern on 26 December 1911.

any of the Chamber-Plays (with the possible exception of *The Ghost Sonata*) and which he therefore did not group with them, his very last dramatic work *The Great Highway (Stora Landsvägen,* 1909).[1]

There were also several plays dating from the last phase of Strindberg's literary productivity with which Intima Teatern had nothing to do. Thus the Arabian Nights entertainment (of German provenance, however) *Abu Casem's Slippers (Abu Casems Tofflor,* 1908) was sold to Karin Swanström's touring company;[2] and *The Last Knight (Siste Riddaren,* 1908), a play about Sten Sture the younger, tossed off at almost incredible speed—Fanny Falkner allows three weeks in one place, only seven days in another—was accepted for production by the Royal Theatre, which had inaugurated its new house in 1908 with a gala performance of the 'verse' *Master Olof.* *The Last Knight* was followed by two more historical dramas which, with it, were designed to complete the great cycle of plays on Swedish history: they are *The Regent (Riksföreståndaren)* in 1908, dealing with Gustav Vasa as a young man before his coronation, and *The Earl of Bjälbo (Bjälbo-Jarlen,* 1909), whose eponymous hero, also called Birger Jarl, was a potentate of the thirteenth century, one of the Folkungs.[3]

The Royal Theatre presented *The Last Knight* (to no very great applause) on Strindberg's sixtieth birthday, 22 January 1909, which Svenska Teatern likewise cele-

[1] Finished and published in 1909, produced 19 February 1910; it takes its name from the road that leads from Nortullsgatan, where he lived as a child, to Nya Kyrkogården, where he rightly presumed he would be buried.

[2] Who presented it at Gävle on 28 December 1908. Strindberg sold his rights for kr. 2000 and spent all the money in one day buying furniture and household equipment for Blå Tornet.

[3] In his last years Strindberg projected a play to serve as pendant to Böcklin's picture, The Island of the Dead, which he greatly admired, and also one with Robespierre as hero.

brated with *Gustavus Vasa*, the Östermalm Theatre in Stockholm with *Lucky Peter's Journey* and Intima Teatern with *There are Crimes and Crimes* in its own house and *Swan-white* at Uppsala. The press, still smarting under its recent castigations, made little of the occasion, but organised labour celebrated the evening by a torchlight procession past Strindberg's windows.

8

These windows no longer faced Karlavägen, but, still in Stockholm, dominated the corner of Drottninggatan and Tegnérgatan. Here stood a house, officially Drottninggatan 85, tall, thin, with blue stairs, to which for these reasons Strindberg gave the name *Blå Tornet*, 'The Blue Tower', into which he moved in July 1908 and where he died a little less than four years later. The neighbours living on the floor above him, the Falkners, a family of Danish origin, looked after him, putting up with that ineradicable distrust of his which now found vent in splenetic accusations of theft and deliberately poisonous cooking, and, when they moved, left their maid Mina to continue as his housekeeper.

Strindberg's isolation from the world, partly imaginary, but chiefly real enough, had increased and, after *Black Banners*, he knew himself once more personally detested and feared. He took his daily exercise, therefore, quite early in the morning, when there was no likelihood of his meeting anyone who might know him in the Stockholm streets, beginning the day's work immediately upon his return to the Blue Tower, at eight o'clock. Thereafter, he wrote, smoked and read at home for the rest of the day; newspapers and periodicals he would never touch, for fear of stumbling upon some uncomplimentary allusion to himself; but he was constantly acquiring new books and kept himself abreast of what was going on, not in the world of literature alone. The casual visitor was severely discouraged by the removal of knocker and bell-pull from his front door and by directions to state his business in the flat one flight up. Schleich records how, wanting to see his old friend again after many years, he overcame these discouragements and, upon repeated thumpings, brought an anxious bloodshot eye to the letter-box slit and heard the stooping genius's muttered ejaculation 'My God! it's Schleich!'[1]

Schleich, nevertheless, did 'effect an entry'. Nor was the Blue Tower always quite so hermetically sealed off from other denizens of the outer world as popular legend had it and its occupant usually liked to make out. The affairs of Intima Teatern demanded frequent consultations with Falck and others, and on occasions the manager with his troupe inveigled the co-director out to a jolly lunch or supper. It is on record that at least once he made a night of it with them at the Lidingöbro Tavern, drinking spirits and playing nine-pins, returned home about the time he usually came in from his constitutional and, after a short rest, sallied forth again to top off with a lobster-luncheon. His elder brother Axel was a constant visitor, and he saw something of his daughters Anne-Marie, Karin and Greta—the latter married to his nephew and physician Henry von Philp. Furthermore, since the great 'Inferno Crisis' he had developed a deeper love of music than he had had before; it quite ousted painting as his principal hobby.[2] He taught

---

[1] *Erinnerungen an Strindberg* (2nd edition, 1917), p. 44.
[2] Strindberg had considerable talents as a painter; quite a number of the pictures which he made between 1870 and 1900 survive: there are

himself to play the pianoforte reasonably well, and a number of his friends—they called themselves collectively, and quite informally, the *Beethoven-gubbarna*, the 'Beethoven-oldsters'—regularly met at his flat for musical evenings.

Lastly, there was the company of Fanny Falkner, one of the daughters of the family upstairs. As a very young art-student, she had taken a small, silent part in *The Ghost Sonata*, on its first presentation in January 1908, and a few weeks later attracted Strindberg's notice at a rehearsal of *Sir Bengt's Wife* in which she was cast as a page. Though she had a weak, twittering voice, he believed that she would realise his ideal of Eleonora in *Easter*, eventually, that autumn, had her put into that part and gave her encouragement and professional advice: he hoped to make a great actress of her. It was through her that he found his Blue Tower, where she came down from the flat overhead every morning to give him secretarial aid and bring him the news of the day, from Intima Teatern in especial. Their mutual affection was tender and great, and, for a very short while, Strindberg, at the age of sixty, and Fanny Falkner, at the age of nineteen, considered themselves engaged to be married. But the anomaly of the relation was too much for them; the vows were tacitly withdrawn; Fröken Falkner left Intima Teatern and, together with her family, No. 85 Drottninggatan; during the last ten months of Strindberg's life, they saw nothing of one another.

coloured reproductions of thirteen of these in Falck, A., *Strindberg och Teatern* (1918). His love of the sea contributed the subjects, which, as he himself admitted, were apt to be all alike—stormy breakers against some torn skerry, with a wild sky and some stunted tree or land-mark.

9

The writings of Strindberg's last years, besides the plays already mentioned, fall mainly into two categories, which however do not quite exclude one another and are completely intermingled in the four consecutive 'Blue Books'. Firstly, there are a number of philological studies (to which much the same criticisms apply as to his scientific speculations), many of them sketched in *A Blue Book* and its successors, but some incorporated also in separate volumes: *Proper Names in the Bible* (*Bibliska Egennamn*, 1910), *The Roots of World-Languages* (*Världs-språkens Rötter*, 1910). *China and Japan* (*Kina och Japan*, 1911) is also largely about the Chinese, Japanese and Tibetan languages,[1] a small number of detachable studies that had first appeared in the Stockholm *Afton-tidningen*. It was, secondly, this new radical newspaper which, in 1910, 1911 and the beginning of 1912, originally printed the majority of Strindberg's last polemical writings,[2] some of which were collected in *Speeches to the Swedish Nation* (*Tal till Svenska Nationen*, 1910), *The Religious Renascence, or Religion versus Theology* (*Religiös Renässans eller Religion mot Teologi*, 1910), *The Popular State* (*Folkstaten*, 1910) and *The Courier of the Czar* (*Czarens Kurir*, 1912).

In the remark that Strindberg's philological and polemical writings could not be rigidly separated the implication was intended that, when he chose, Strindberg could be as controversial about philology as about any other subject. Nevertheless, the tone of his polemics, whatever the field, had changed. The religious belief in

---

[1] There was a substantial supplement to this book in *The Provenance of the Chinese Language* (*Kinesiska Språkets Härkomst*, 1912).

[2] Others appeared in *Social-Demokraten* as well as in the 'Blue Books'.

resignation and tolerance, so long and often so incon-
gruously professed, seemed on the way to becoming a
genuine personal creed, though it was a slow process:
he was indulgent and charitable to the poor; he showed
innumerable attentions to the relatives and others who
were still admitted to his intimacy; he craved to do right,
to see life beautiful, to have sympathy with men—'but
I cannot respect them, cannot love them, for I know them
through myself'. Strindberg was a believing Christian, a
fundamentalist shot with Swedenborgian allegory, unable on the one hand to accept the 'confession' of Augs-
burg or, indeed, of any one sect, hostile on the other
hand to submitting the foundations of Christianity to
the researches of the philologists and the constructions
of the doctors. He reverenced and even endeavoured to
follow the teaching of the Gospels, but, till his end, his
God still presumably continued to be the God of the
Old Testament[1]; 'Jehovah! Hey!' he had piously ex-
claimed as he was shaking off his atheism, 'That is the
God for me—an eye for an eye, an ear for an ear [*sic*]!'

His re-entry into the political arena, more than a
quarter of a century after *The New State*, was due in all
probability to two causes.[2] One was the mounting opposition to the conservative government that had risen
to power in 1906, exasperating Strindberg's instinctive
itch to discredit authority and majority opinion. He had
never understood the aristocratic (as distinct from the
Nietzschean or the feudal)[3] view of life and had always
execrated the 'matadors' of business, as they are called

---

[1] He confessed that he could not understand the Christian doctrine of
the Atonement and presumably did not accept it.
[2] For foreign audiences he had championed the cause of Norwegian
separation from Sweden in *Ein freies Norwegen* (Leipzig, 1905).
[3] This does not necessarily imply that Strindberg interpreted these
views of life quite reliably either.

in the North, who, with their satellites, controlled so much of middle-class politics. The great labour leader Hjalmar Branting was an old friend, and now Strindberg came forward as the mouthpiece of working-class aspirations, including in his sympathies the urban proletariat for the first time. The social democrats, according to his new programme, were not to annihilate or even altogether to ruin the rest, but they were to secure complete political and fiscal power and use it to their profit against landed property, big business, even the Crown itself. Hence the phenomenon of a torchlight procession of trade unionists to salute the author of such esoteric products as *Black Banners* and *The Ghost Sonata*.

Even in his most benevolent hours, however, Strindberg was seldom able to forget himself, his 'honour' and the position which he felt should rightfully be his in the world. A second reason for the socialistic agitation of his last four years is bound up with the *crise d'indignation* from which *Black Banners* had emanated. Conspicuous to his view among those who denied his claim to literary greatness, were what might be described as the aristocratic, aesthetising faction under the critic Levertin[1] and his old associate Verner von Heidenstam[2] (who set up their Ivory Tower over against his Blue Tower and labelled as 'barbarism' the lunacies, horrors, superstitions, violence, and formlessness of his writing), and the Swedish Academy of Literature, the very citadel, he believed, of hide-bound conservatism in all matters of the spirit. A special grudge he bore the Academy was their withholding from him the Nobel

[1] Who died in 1906.
[2] Heidenstam pronounced Strindberg to be 'the full-blooded barbarian in our literature.... The virtues of civilisation he detests with heart and soul.... Strindberg, with his icy grey, suspicious look from underneath is a runaway serf' (cit. Hedén, p. 428).

Prize for Literature, which he thought rightfully due to him (but for which under the terms of the benefaction he was scarcely eligible).

For the latter reason it was that he gave the name 'Anti-Nobel Prize' to the nation-wide monetary testimonial[1] which was raised for his behoof in anticipation of his 'grand climacteric,' his sixty-third birthday, celebrated (though not by everybody) with a good deal more enthusiasm and harmony than had invested the commemoration of his sixtieth birthday. There was a procession past his house and five special performances of his plays in the capital that evening.

By this time, however, Strindberg was a sick man. He had long suspected serious stomachic trouble, and, late in the winter of 1911–12, it was diagnosed as cancer. He died, after great sufferings, at 4.30 in the afternoon of 14 May 1912, clasping to his breast the Bible with which he was buried.

One passes by as quickly as possible the odious hypocrisy and disregard of Strindberg's express wishes made manifest at the interment in the Nya Kyrkogården of Stockholm five days later and the equally revolting vandalism which took advantage of a public holiday to rob the new grave of its floral tributes. Only the Swedish Academy maintained its dignity, treating the dead man with the same sovereign disdain that it had shown, in life, to the greatest Swedish writer of his day.

---

[1] Like almost all the public activities with which Strindberg was associated, the raising of this testimonial had its grotesque aspects: no substantial citizen, for instance, could be found to act as treasurer of the fund. The appeal, moreover, was somewhat hampered by the knowledge that Strindberg had just concluded a lucrative contract with the great publishing firm of Bonnier for the collection of his writings, *Samlade Skrifter*, which began to appear in 1911. The testimonial amounted to kr. 45,000, all of which Strindberg gave away, determined, according to his principles, to live by his royalties alone.

"Strindberg as seen by

a naturalist.

a darwinist,   a symbolist."

Caricature by Oskar Andersson.

CHAPTER V

THE PLAYS

I

IT has been said that Norwegian literature is mainly dramatic, Danish literature mainly epic, and Swedish literature mainly lyric. One need not, perhaps, go so far as to maintain that Sweden has no real story-tellers of epic breadth, yet a foreigner, approaching Swedish literature for the first time, can hardly fail to be surprised by the scarcity of any plays worth the name—until he realises that the economic and social framework, which in England conditioned, if it does not altogether explain, the genius of Shakespeare and the flowering of the Elizabethan dramatists, and in France called forth the measured cadences of Racinian tragedy and allowed the penetrating criticisms of Molière, was simply an impossibility in the primitive Sweden of the sixteenth and seventeenth centuries.

Thus there was no golden age in Swedish drama, though of course plays were written and produced, at first moralities, then crude tragedies, and masques, the latter more particularly under the patronage of Queen Kristina (1636–54), who desired to imitate the courtly fashions of France in this respect as in others. Foreign actors, first Dutch and German, then Italian and French, visited Sweden, and during the eighteenth century, indeed, Stockholm enjoyed the benefits of a professional French company—with some interruptions. These activities were supplemented by amateur performances at Court, both in French and Swedish. No permanent Swedish company was established, however, until 1737, when Bollhuset (The Tennis Court) was made available to a troupe of students and civil servants; a somewhat similar Swedish company, made up of Uppsala students, had acted during the years 1686–91 at Lejonkulan (The Lion's Den), a building originally erected to house a lion bestowed on Queen Kristina. By 1691 these students had been ousted by a German company, who maintained themselves there until the building was burnt down in 1697. Even the company at Bollhuset, or Kungliga Svenska Skådeplatsen (The Royal Swedish Stage), as it was called, fell upon evil days towards the middle of the eighteenth century. The low standard of the fare offered is revealed by the comment of Lovisa Ulrika (then Crown Princess, later Queen, of Sweden), the brilliant sister of Frederick the Great of Prussia, who wrote: 'I found so little pleasure in it that I never in my life wish to return there. The platitudes went on for four hours. No possibility of leaving, owing to the mob that barred the passage out.'

Nor did Gustavus III (1771–92), with all his lively interest in drama and acting (hostile critics have called him an actor in real life), succeed in creating a living Swedish theatrical tradition, though, both through his patronage of the Royal Opera (Kungliga Operan) and through his own theatre at Drottningholm Castle, he did much to increase the prestige of dramatic activities in Sweden. But the original Swedish works performed under his aegis, including those which he wrote himself, were at best second-rate pseudo-classical imitations of foreign models.

The Romantic Movement (Nyromantiken), unlike its prototype in France, did not produce any actable plays of literary value, though Atterbom's verse drama

The Isle of Bliss (Lycksalighetens Ö), and some of Alm-quist's efforts, achieved a high poetical standard. Bern-hard von Beskow is the most respectable exponent of the kind of Romantic historical play which became popular with Swedish audiences in the 'sixties. With the con-tinued and steady growth of foreign literary influences, and the availability to Swedish readers of foreign texts, either in the original or in translation, for instance Shakespeare,[1] Goethe, Schiller, Tieck, as well as the French Romantics and the succeeding generation of French playwrights, Scribe, Augier, Dumas *fils*, to-gether with contemporary Danish and Norwegian writers,[2] and with the steady economic and commercial development of Sweden, marked here, as in other Euro-pean countries, by the rise of the middle classes and the corresponding demand for entertainment, it was only natural that in Sweden, too, by the 1850's and 1860's, the theatre should have become an established institu-tion, in spite of the dearth of any outstanding native talent.

Meanwhile, original Swedish plays were, of course, produced. Such dramas as Frans Hedberg's *The Mar-riage at Ulvåsa (Bröllopet på Ulvåsa)* and August Blanche's *The Girl in the Stadsgård (Flickan i Stadsgården)* were ex-tremely popular. It was only to later and more detached readers that their essential mediocrity became over-whelmingly apparent. It was in *The Marriage at Ulvåsa*, but only at a rehearsal, that Strindberg was allowed to attempt a part in 1869, and was driven by this and other failures, like the Dane, Hans Andersen, before him, to seek another outlet for his creative talents. We have no

[1] Hagberg's translations appeared between 1847 and 1851.
[2] The Danes, Hertz, Hauch, and Hostrup may be mentioned especi-ally, as well as the Norwegians, Bjørnson and Ibsen.

means of knowing whether Strindberg, if he had perse-
vered, would ever have had the makings of a good actor:
judged on the basis of his character, it seems improbable. Strindberg himself attributed his failure to his
infringement of the accepted technical conventions. He
did not, and would not, declaim blank verse in the slow
pompous manner laid down at the Royal Theatre for
the Swedish historical dramas as well as for the numer-
ous performances of Shakespearean chronicle plays
and tragedies, Schiller, Œhlenschläger, Bjørnson's and
Ibsen's historical plays—a manner of diction enforced
even for the bourgeois comedies in prose which delighted
the more vulgar audiences at the Nya Teatern (New
Theatre). When the plays of Augier and Sardou were
produced at Stockholm in the modern French manner,
that is in the tempo of everyday life, the innovation
caused an outcry. I have dwelt on these details as indi-
cating the character of the Swedish stage of the 'sixties,
a decade which became known and commemorated in
the pages of contemporary memoirs for the excellence of
its actors rather than of its playwrights.

2

It was within these narrow limits of matter and manner
that Strindberg was first to try his wings as a dramatist
in his real *début* as writer. Yet in his earliest attempt at
drama now extant, *The Freethinker* (*Fritänkaren*), composed in 1869, Strindberg had the courage to treat in a
contemporary setting a serious subject, the conflict in
the mind of the young man, Karl, between the calls of
conscience and the compromises and conventions imposed by society. In Scandinavian terms Strindberg was
here not a pioneer, for echoes of Ibsen's *Brand* clearly

resound in the hero's condemnation of any feeble concessions to society: 'The last link which still held me has been loosened; now I stand alone in the fight, but with the Lord as my shield.'[1] Karl's truculence and aggressiveness in his search for truth doubtless also reflect Strindberg's own failure to adjust himself to the life around him. Like Strindberg at this period, Karl is an earnest disciple of Parker's Unitarianism, and this faith provides the focal point in the otherwise slight work, clumsily and inexpertly handled, but not without potentialities. To contemporary opinion it was not acceptable. It was published under a pseudonym in 1870, and condemned by the critics, whose harsh strictures drove Strindberg back within the conventional field. Whilst his hero, Karl, proclaimed that he intended to emigrate to America in order to preach the truth there, Strindberg went on to write *Hermione*, a tragedy in five acts in Schillerian style, the theme of which is the conquest of Athens by Philip of Macedon, Demosthenes, the Athenian champion of freedom, being betrayed by the cowardly apathy of his own people.

Of the two other apprentice works written during 1870–1, *In Rome* (*I Rom*) and *The Outlaw* (*Den Fredlöse*), the verse play *In Rome* makes the slighter impression. Not because of the theme, which is that of the artist's doubts concerning his vocation, but owing to the *naïveté* and superficiality with which it is treated. The hero, the young Thorvaldsen, who is struggling in Rome for recognition as a sculptor, has obvious personal links with Strindberg, voicing the author's own questionings of himself and his call in life. In *The Outlaw*, Strindberg moved even further away from contemporary events than he had done in *Hermione*, and, under the influence

[1] *Samlade Skrifter* (subsequently given as *S.S.*), I, 41.

(as he later admitted) of Bjørnson and Ibsen, as well as of Œhlenschläger, selected an ancient Icelandic subject, the conflict between Paganism and the new Christianity, as it unfolds itself in one particular family, that of Thorfinn. In the style of *The Outlaw* was reflected the modern Norwegian conception—and exaggeration—of Icelandic taciturnity (Strindberg had of course read the Icelandic Sagas), so that, in the writer's desire to achieve concentration, the speech of the characters often becomes extraordinarily obscure. Though a note of harmony is sounded at the end, when the dying pagan Thorfinn is reconciled to his family and to the new faith, the atmosphere in general is one of heavy gloom. In these first attempts Strindberg was evidently fumbling among existing forms for a dramatic formula which should appeal to the public and yet satisfy his own artistic standards. Very little in them seems to foreshadow the mastery revealed in the next play, *Master Olof* (*Mäster Olof*).

3

For a young man of twenty-three, *Master Olof* is a remarkable achievement. I consider, indeed, that, viewed from any angle, the play is noteworthy and effective; after the lapse of almost seventy years it has dated very little in comparison with most of the literature of that decade, and retains its freshness and power. It deals with the Reformation in Sweden, in the reign of Gustav Vasa, the hero Olof being the actual historical personage who, under the direction of the King, did so much, both politically and spiritually, to further the cause of the new religion in Sweden. Olof, who, when the action begins, is still a young priest, teaching at the Cathedral school at Strängnäs, is called to the task of spreading the

95

new doctrines in the country. Full of youthful idealism and zeal, he accepts the call and preaches to the people of the diocese at a time when the Bishop has forbidden any such spiritual succour, because the tithes have not been paid. When Bishop Brask of Linköping, the strongest representative of the Established Church in Sweden, and other dignitaries threaten to punish the young rebel, Gustav Vasa intervenes, appoints him secretary to Stockholms Rådstuga (Stockholm Law Courts), and despatches him to preach to the people of the capital. That is, the King has chosen him as an instrument with which to oppose the Papal power, which threatens the King's political rule; but Gustav Vasa intends also that Olof shall curb the more extreme religious reformers, of whom Gert the Printer, the Anabaptist, is the most dangerous representative.

Olof, though excommunicated by the Catholic Church, does preach to the citizens, but goes further than the King wishes him to do, in his sincere belief that the abuses of Catholicism threaten the human soul with perdition: he thus rouses the conservative citizens to the pitch of stoning him. Only Kristina, Gert's daughter, who, in spite of her father's extreme views, has, by his own wish, been brought up as an orthodox Catholic and in ignorance of any dissident faith, stands by Olof, because of her instinctively deep emotional feelings for him. His mother, representative of the old, unquestioning beliefs, tries to pull him back within the fold, fails, and leaves him. Olof marries Kristina, thereby further outraging public opinion, with the result that she is treated as a harlot by Olof's mother and by the common people.

Through his preaching, nevertheless, Olof has assisted the King in making the Reformation possible. It is because the King needs him, that he is allowed to continue, though he is warned that he must in future restrain his violence. At the meeting of the Estates at Västerås (1527) the Reformation is carried through as a political measure, that is, the King is empowered to confiscate a considerable proportion of Church property; he can thus restore the unsound finances of the country, and, furthermore, check the militant arrogance of the bishops. The new decrees, however, do not enforce the preaching of the new faith. Thus, at the very moment of triumph—he has been appointed rector of Storkyrkan (The Great Church) in Stockholm in reward for his services—Olof is cautioned, by the nobleman who brings him the King's message, that he must not touch the old religious rites. He then realises the truth which Gert has been urging on him from the beginning, that he cannot serve both God and King. He is persuaded by Gert to conspire against the King, the logical step to take, so it seems to him now, when the King provides the only obstacle to the new faith. Meanwhile Olof's mother dies, cursing her son, who refuses to let her be succoured on her death-bed by the rites of the Catholic Church. She is the first victim of the plague that has swept into Stockholm, and her death is interpreted by the people as a sign of God's condemnation of her son's heresy. Gert now informs Olof of what he has been planning, and reveals, what Olof had not realised, that the King's death must be the next step in the plot.

Now, however, the conspiracy is betrayed by the bibulous Windrank, one of the humbler instruments of the league, whose assistance has been bought with bribes, and who talks in his cups. Ironically enough, it is Kristina, unaware of her husband's part in the plot, who assists in giving the alarm.

97

In the final scene of the play (there are five acts) the conspirators have been caught, and Gert and Olof sit on stools of repentance inside Storkyrkan, awaiting execution. Lars, Olof's brother, who throughout the play is portrayed as representing the more conciliatory aspect of the Reformation movement, is deputed by the King to offer Olof a pardon, on condition that he recants. The old Lord High Constable puts the King's views formally, but in pleading with Olof uses the weight of his own experience: 'I too have been young, and have been spurred on by violent passions; that is a part of youth, but these passions are intended to be suppressed',[1] and 'You should have shed your dreams rather earlier.'[2] Conscious of his youth and his vitality, and now shaken in his belief that his version of the truth is the only one, Olof recants. As he stands in the church after this recantation, there enters one of his former pupils from Strängnäs, Vilhelm, a boy who has throughout continued to look up to him, and has now come to thank him for his example of enduring fortitude, and for his gift of freedom. After this ironic comment on Olof's behaviour, there resounds, as the final word in the play, the farewell uttered by Gert, when he is led out to his death: 'Renegade!'

In this play, then, Gert speaks for the inflexible revolutionary spirit. In a sense he is the hero, as much as Olof, or more so, a fact which weakens the play technically, whilst giving it a wider ideological range. When Strindberg wrote the play, he was already on the way to becoming an atheist; thus the religious theme does not interest him primarily, but rather the *motif* of revolution in and for itself, the burden of Gert's speech in the last scene, which begins: 'Our harvest was not ripe...cen-

[1] *S.S.* II, 181.   [2] *S.S.* II, 181.

turies will pass before even a shoot is visible';[1] not the survival of one religious faith or another, but the question of the survival of any principles whatever. The fact that Strindberg selected a historical framework for his modern problem was no doubt partly due to the example of predecessors such as Schiller and his contemporary Ibsen; partly it may be ascribed to his own earlier failure, with *The Freethinker*, in dealing with a modern theme in a modern setting.

In the first place his inspiration for such a treatment of history is derived from Shakespeare. Strindberg wrote later[2] that the work was inspired by *Julius Caesar*[3], but one is actually much more impressed by its resemblance to *Henry IV* and occasionally to *Hamlet*. Strindberg has not, however, let himself be dominated by the Schillerian conception of Shakespeare; it was Georg Brandes' interpretation of the Elizabethan, with its emphasis on Shakespeare's use of realistic detail, that fired his imagination. The description, for instance, of the habits of the monks Mårten and Nils, becomes the epitome of the corruption of the Catholic Church. The motley scenes of revelry in the tavern (Act II), which is situated in the very wall of Storkyrkan, serve as a foil to the solemn proceedings in the church itself. Like Shakespeare again, Strindberg uses the device of introducing representatives of various nationalities (like Fluellen in *Henry V*), in the person of the Dane and the German, to give life and colour to his background. In the Shakespearean chronicle plays Strindberg would also have found the apparently loose construction of tableaux, though in fact the seemingly casual shifts of scene in

---

[1] *S.S.* II, 179.   [2] *S.S.* L, 123.
[3] For Strindberg's debt to Shakespeare see J. Bulman, *Strindberg and Shakespeare* (1933).

Master Olof conceal a not inconsiderable dramatic skill. Strindberg pointed out later in his autobiography *In the Red Room* (*I Röda Rummet*) that Goethe's *Götz von Berlichingen*, which of course itself represented Goethe's own response to the liberating technique of Shakespeare, had served as model here.

Much the most interesting and important debt to Shakespeare (but it cannot be explained simply as such) is the bold treatment of history as material to be chopped about by the dramatist for his own purposes, so that he may transform historical personages into beings who are really his own creations, and telescope years into months or even days. From the standpoint of pedantic scholarship, *Master Olof* does not rank as history; but, in its isolation of certain ideas and the emphasis laid upon them, the play does turn a certain cross-section of the sixteenth century into living history.

Strindberg succeeds in this partly by creating characters that live in spite of, or rather because of, their inconsistency: they are modern, many of them, people of Strindberg's own period, with their complicated approach to problems of faith. Olof himself, in whom are mirrored so many of the young Strindberg's own doubts and fears, impulses and acts of will, conflicts with his family and ambitions, differs considerably from the accepted portrait of the original. The final effect left on the reader by this play is one of confusion as to its 'message'; yet this fact in itself, while detracting from the work's slickness, endows it with a richer texture. I do not wish to press the analogy too far, but in this provocative obscurity *Master Olof* bears some resemblance to *Hamlet*. Just as *Hamlet*, too, contains within its framework the tricks of the Elizabethan melodrama, so *Master Olof* is marred (see for instance the conspiracy and the role of Gert) by obvious loans from the technique of recent French dramatists, Scribe and most probably Sardou.

Strindberg achieved his freshness of treatment largely by his handling of prose dialogue, his racy, even coarse, vocabulary, which in concentration and liveliness bore little relation to the conventional language of the Swedish stage. He was to go to much greater extremes in some of his later historical plays, in the use of outspoken language (as well as of anachronistic detail), but nowhere are force and lyricism more happily married than in *Olof*.

The rejection of *Master Olof*, and the criticism it received, drove Strindberg to rewrite it—in fact we know that even before the rejection he was considering another version, but clearly the tone of the criticisms affected the form of the subsequent attempts. The verse play, in Strindberg's effort to make it approximate more closely to the demands of Dramaten, has lost some of the freshness and liveliness of the prose version. The changes in it, however, also reflect a development in Strindberg's views, that conviction of the relativity of all truth which the reading of Buckle and others[1] had implanted in him, and which already makes itself felt in the prose version, though in a much less clear-cut way.

In the later version Olof has a far more important part than the revolutionary Gert, whose role is now secondary. King Gustav does not appear at all; the Lord High Constable speaks for him, and, at the end, when Olof is faced with the problem whether to recant or die, he (the Constable) and Bishop Brask each present one aspect of the truth. Olof at first refuses to recant because of his vows to Luther at Wittenberg, but

[1] See above, Chapter I, p. 22.

the Constable then appears and reads a letter from
Luther to the German Princes: 'If twice two are four
but the Emperor says they make five, then five it is.'[1] In
the final scene, after Olof has asked for mercy, the
scholar Vilhelm comes, as in the prose work, to say farewell to him, and it is Vilhelm, not Gert, who cries
'Renegade'. But Strindberg does not allow him the last
word; instead, Olof expresses his relief at having survived the storm. The verse itself, chiefly rhymed doggerel (certain scenes are still in prose), helps to give a
more formal, detached feeling to the conflict. Strindberg has also sacrificed certain scenes to economy of construction: for instance, those in the inn have been
omitted. Instead, a careful exposition in the first act depicts Olof's horrified reactions to the corruption, sloth,
and gluttony of the Catholic Church as personified in
the fat Confessor and Beldenacke. At the same time,
Mårten, who in the prose version represented the most
vicious aspects of the Church, has been transformed, in
the verse play, into a humorous, almost jovial, character. Thus Strindberg shows himself here in more
tolerant mood.

This tolerance, and the better equilibrium which explains it, were caused by the great change in Strindberg's life marked by his love for Siri von Essen and the
temporary improvement in his financial circumstances.
His feelings for Siri von Essen reflect themselves, for instance, in the lyrical passages of the scene (Act IV, Scene
iv), where Olof sits by his mother's death-bed and sees
dawn break over Stockholm. It may also be safely
assumed that his love for Siri deepened and also complicated his conception of the relationship between Olof
and Kristina, which, however, may be based in part on

[1] *S.S.* II, 303.

a previous erotic experience. Kristina would like to be everything to Olof; she realises that she is not his intellectual equal, resents his work in a way, would like to humble him, and yet at the same time looks up to him. When Olof is too busy to devote much time to her, she transfers her love to the child whom she has borne him. Only the disaster threatening Olof reunites them. Here are already in embryo the disharmonious relations between man and woman, as Strindberg was to depict them so often in later writings. The fact that Kristina is presented as the rather more attractive personality of the two may be partly explained by Strindberg's desire, at this time, to please Siri von Essen.

The verse play, too, was rejected by Dramaten. Strindberg finally published it in 1878 after adding an 'Epilogue', in which he gave vent to his renewed cynicism. Master Olof here appears after the lapse of many years as an aged, fat, red-nosed cleric, a very pillar of society.

4

On account of his almost obsessional rewriting of *Olof*, Strindberg was diverted from the realistic drama, which he might at this time have been developing in Scandinavia, and so, as he bitterly complained later, this task was meanwhile taken up by Bjørnson in Norway. From the point of view of production, these years appear to form a sterile period in Strindberg's life. He afterwards explained the origin of his next group of plays in his slanderous autobiography *A Madman's Defence* (*Le Plaidoyer d'un Fou* or *En Dåres Försvarstal*) as the desire to provide his wife with attractive parts (Siri and he having married at the end of 1877). This may be taken as an exaggeration of a kind typical of Strindberg; for financial reasons, in any case, would have compelled him to write, and he probably continued with the genre of historical plays because as yet he felt uncertain about his power of handling realistic drama and still hoped that his works would be produced at Dramaten.

The Secret of the Guild (*Gillets Hemlighet*) written in 1879–80, set in the fifteenth century, has as theme the rivalry between Sten, the able and true architect, and Jacques, the worthless and dishonest one, for the honour of completing the cathedral at Uppsala. Here once more the historical subject becomes a vehicle for modern ideas: it is the vocation of the poet which is symbolised by the building of the cathedral, and in this symbolisation Strindberg, who saw himself as Sten, had certainly been influenced by Ibsen's *Pretenders* (*Kongsemnerne*), in which Skule steals the idea of kingship from Håkon Jarl. The next historical play, *Sir Bengt's Wife* (*Herr Bengts Hustru*), completed in the autumn of 1882, again has a medieval setting. Margit is saved from the convent by Bengt, who marries her. Their state of bliss does not last long. Soon, as in Strindberg's own marriage, bitter quarrels develop. Bengt keeps his wife in ignorance of his economic difficulties; Margit, in her youthful romanticism and inexperience of life, lets herself be absorbed by the beauties, rather than the practical problems, of life. Yet, at the crisis in the couple's affairs, it is Margit who tackles the practical problems and tries to save their fortunes. After some extremely melodramatic incidents, including attempted suicide by poison, the young pair are reconciled. This play may be considered as Strindberg's first endeavour in literature to discuss the questions raised by Ibsen's *Doll's House* (*Et Dukkehjem*). Strindberg, as is well known, became a bitter critic of Ibsen's views, yet in *Sir Bengt's Wife* he is, on the whole, less prejudiced than usual in his own (i.e. the hero's) favour, and Bengt's violence, jealousy, and difficult temperament are admitted to be causes of the domestic conflict.

For the third play of this period, *Lucky Peter's Journey* (*Lycko-Pers Resa*), written in 1882, Strindberg chose the fairy-tale form rather than the historical. In this he was influenced both by Atterbom's *The Isle of Bliss* and by Hans Andersen's stories, not to mention Ibsen's *Peer Gynt*, and Œhlenschläger's *Aladdin*. In spite of the derivative nature of its conception, the play has an attractive freshness. The hero, Per, possesses a magic ring which gives him the power of wishing and having his wishes granted; with the help of the ring he proceeds from one disillusioning experience to another, until some of the selfishness is knocked out of him by life and he is finally redeemed by the agency of the girl Lisa. Strindberg is still struggling to maintain the mood of reconciliation which inspired the happy ending of *The Secret of the Guild* and survived in *Sir Bengt's Wife*; nevertheless the satire on society, much the most interesting aspect of the play, sounds a very bitter note. As in the contemporary *New State*, Strindberg castigates the corrupt intrigues of Swedish demagogy and his contemporaries' fear of any real reform for the good of the whole state.

5

During the next phase of his life with Siri von Essen, when he was moving from place to place in Germany, Switzerland and France, Strindberg's dramatic production lapsed at first entirely. Increasingly absorbed in sociological research, he tended to despise *belles lettres* as such. To his mind the drama was more conventional in form, and therefore more reprehensible, than the novel or the short story: the contemporary form of drama had not yet proved itself on a level with these *genres* as a vehicle for ideas, though Strindberg, in his sharply worded critiques[1] of modern French comedy, that is, comedy in the style of Dumas *fils* and of Sardou, acknowledged the contributions made by Bjørnson and Ibsen towards developing the scope of the theatre.

The Camp-Followers (*Marodörerna*), started in 1886, then rewritten and published in 1888 under the title of *The Comrades* (*Kamraterna*), represents Strindberg's first direct treatment of a contemporary theme (apart from *The Freethinker*), and was planned as a satirical comedy, to make fun of the emancipation of women; but, while Strindberg was writing it, the theme of his own conflict with his wife entangled itself with the lines of this plot, and the tone became increasingly bitter. He planned, while in Denmark (in 1888), to run a Scandinavian theatre, at which his wife could act and his own plays could be produced, and this idea, of course, in its turn, provided a stimulus to him as dramatic author; but the whole plan must have originated just in the very fact of his irrepressible need to write plays, in spite of all his scientific theories to the contrary. The heroine of *The Camp-Followers* is a painter like her husband, but, whereas he can paint, she cannot. At the end, Bertha, who, like her husband Axel, has sent in a picture to the Salon (the setting is Paris), is busy preparing to celebrate her triumph, in that her picture has been accepted, his refused, when the truth is suddenly revealed: only Axel's chivalry is responsible for her name being on the list; it is his picture which has been accepted. *The Comrades*— another rejoinder to Ibsen's *Doll's House*—has a more

[1] E.g., in *S.S.* xvii, 234–45, 281–303.

brutal ending: Bertha is turned out of the house. But in both plays the essential theme is the clash between man and woman, the matter of the much more interesting and effective play *The Father* (*Fadren*). Clearly Strindberg's obsession with his own experiences drove him to dramatise them.

The Father provides interesting evidence of the rapidity with which Strindberg could work. He planned it at the end of 1886, began writing it in the New Year of 1887, and seems to have finished it by the end of February—a marked contrast to the deliberate process of incubation practised by Ibsen. It appears to have been planned as part of an uncompleted trilogy, for Bertha, the young daughter in *The Father*, had appeared as the heroine of the play already discussed above. The hero, the Captain (Ryttmästaren), is goaded into madness by his wife, Laura, who wantonly sows doubts in his mind as to the paternity of their daughter. It is the daughter who becomes, however unwittingly, the cause of their struggle for power. The Captain, who is represented as a highly nervous, and therefore suggestible, but intelligent and sharp-witted man (Strindberg clearly attaches considerable importance to his intelligence, describing him as a well-known scientist), does not employ any unfair methods. He loves his daughter, loves her too ardently; Laura, on the other hand, appears completely unscrupulous in her determination to obtain legal control over the girl. By first suggesting that her daughter is illegitimate, then maintaining that there is no crime which a mother would not commit, then swearing that he is the father of Bertha, she plunges her husband into such a confusion of doubts and suspicions that he does not know what to accept, what to reject. Thus doubt, rather than belief in his wife's unfaithfulness, forms the driving force in the Captain's downfall. Laura then deals him a further blow: she tells him that she is arranging to have him put in a lunatic asylum. Maddened by her ruses, he throws a burning lamp at her head, an act which provides sufficient grounds for his wife to have him certified, especially as she has already won over the new district doctor to her side.

In the last scenes the Captain is shown with the Old Nurse, who cajoles him into a strait jacket and takes away from him the revolver with which he had intended to commit suicide. In this terrible and pitiful situation he has his final reckoning with Laura, and immediately afterwards collapses in a fit. In this act the Captain rises to a really tragic stature in the catastrophe which overwhelms him, in his resignation in the face thereof, and in his half-crazed, half-rapt memories of the first happy days of his marriage. One may criticise Strindberg for setting this character in a military milieu, when his nature is so devoid of military toughness, but for the rest, considered as a portrait, he convinces and moves. Strindberg's own fears and doubts had been woven into the texture; doubts as to the paternity of his children, fears as to his own madness, as well as his reading of works on suggestion and hypnotism.

In *The Father* Strindberg deliberately attempted to write a modern Greek tragedy on a sort of Agamemnon-and-Clytemnestra theme. This led him back to the simplicity of the dramatic unities, the whole action taking place within twenty-four hours, in one room, and a very small number of characters—eight—being introduced. In following this pattern, Strindberg was also approximating to what the French Naturalists, especially Zola, wished to achieve in drama, that is, concentration on milieu and psychological interest at the expense of plot. As early as 1880, in his essay *Le naturalisme au théâtre*, Zola had laid down his programme for that theatre, but it is probable that Strindberg had not read this until after he had finished *The Father*. Yet, while Strindberg goes further than Ibsen in his realistic and brutal portrayal of madness on the stage, he does not overload the play with scientific details, in the way in which Zola crowded his novels with paraphernalia. In spite, too, of inconsistencies in character-drawing, and his obviously prejudiced approach to the conflict, Strindberg's handling of technique in this play is brilliant, more particularly in his use of dialogue with its concentration and its simultaneously casual allusiveness.

The play was translated into French, Zola wrote a preface for it, and Antoine, at the Théâtre Libre, accepted it for production. This sudden brightening of his prospects awakened in Strindberg the hope of becoming a writer of European fame, and of setting a fashion for Scandinavian literature comparable to that already existing for Russian. His next two plays, *Lady Julia (Fröken Julie)* and *Creditors (Fordringsägare)*, were written with the Théâtre Libre in mind. This experimental theatre, in accordance with the naturalist acceptance of the unities, began to abolish curtain drops, thus eliminating any division into acts. In *Lady Julia* the break in the action between the first and second parts is punctuated by the entry of the dancing peasants, who toss off their midsummer *snaps* or punch, and then dance off again. The subject of the play is the seduction of Lady Julia, the count's daughter, by the valet Jean, or, as one might equally well put it, the seduction of Jean by Lady Julia. The action takes place one midsummer eve in the kitchen of the count's house, and Kristin the cook is the only other character. She is

Jean's girl-friend; with her solid common-sense vulgarity she acts as an effective foil to the hysterical exaltation of Lady Julia and to the naïve, half-baked, sophistications of Jean; there is something typically Swedish in her abrupt yet formal manner, her imperturbable conviction of her own righteousness and efficiency, whether she is preparing a platter of food for the bitch, or commenting on her mistress's downfall.

The action moves to the climax of the seduction. Lady Julia and the valet, driven out of the kitchen by the crowding yokels, take refuge in Jean's room. The second half of the play, after the disappearance of the dancers and the re-entry of Jean and Julia, is, so to speak, a reaction against the events of the first part. The inevitable reversal of Julia's emotions after the seduction is intensified by her discovery that Jean is coarser and more contemptible than she had imagined. She and Jean make plans to escape abroad and start a hotel, but have no money to finance such a venture. Sitting there in the early hours of the morning, in the stuffy kitchen, which the yokels have left in disorder, and drinking wine, Jean becomes more and more wounding and coarse in his comments on her, which are the antithesis of his earlier poetical wooing, whilst she, further excited by the wine, starts confessing to him her own and her family's secrets. She is in a state of hysteria, which alternates between a kind of frenzied exaltation and apathetic hopelessness. Jean meanwhile simply gets sleepier and more bored as the time passes. She then implores him to will her to get ready for flight, and disappears, to provide herself with funds from her father's desk.

In her absence, Kristin enters, dressed for church, and soon guesses what has happened. Her comment expresses the opinion of the ordinary domestic servant on such infringements of the social code: 'No, really. I won't stop in this house any longer, where one can't respect one's betters.'[1] When Kristin has gone out, after Jean has agreed to accompany her to church, Lady Julia returns, as the sun rises, and persuades Jean to go with her on her flight. Kristin, however, returns in time to catch them in the act of departing. Julia, by now in the last stages of hysteria, rapidly sketches a new plan by which Kristin shall join forces with them in the hotel business, but is crushed by Kristin's question: 'Do you really believe in that yourself?'[2] Kristin now departs on a wave of pious smugness, after first warning them that she will make escape impossible by telling the groom not to let them have any horses. Julia sinks down utterly exhausted, and picks up Jean's razor. Suicide seems to her the only way out, yet she lacks the willpower to perform the act. The sudden ringing of the bell in the kitchen announces the master's return. Jean, from being the nonchalant seducer, is transformed back into the obsequious servant. Julia, of course, realises that her theft will now be discovered, and considers that death is the only alternative to dishonour. She implores Jean to order her, to hypnotise her, so that she may go out to the barn to kill herself, and the last incident in this very skilfully and subtly modulated drama is Julia's disappearance through the door with the razor in her hand.

The story, of the most ordinary kind, Strindberg had actually heard related (with a different ending) in Sweden several years before, but *mutatis mutandis* it could easily be more or less paralleled by many paragraphs in the more sensational Sunday papers. Zola

[1] *S.S.* xxiii, 169.   [2] *S.S.* xxiii, 179.

desired that the drama should prove the universal validity of those laws, heredity and the influence of environment, which he intended his own novels to illustrate. Strindberg takes the hereditary elements in the two main characters, the degenerate streak in Lady Julia, and the 'climber' psychology of the plebeian valet, and makes them into the mainsprings of the plot, but not the only springs. He wishes to stress the multiplicity of the motives which govern every human action.

In the Preface to *Lady Julia*, which was written after the play itself, and, incidentally, reflects the influence upon him of his reading of Nietzsche,[1] Strindberg points out what he has tried to achieve in this work, in a passage worth quoting: 'Lady Julia's tragic fate has been ascribed by me to a whole multitude of circumstances: the instincts derived from her mother; the father's faulty upbringing of the girl; her own character and the influence of her *fiancé* on a weak degenerate brain; further, and more directly, the festive mood of Midsummer Eve; her father's absence; her own physical condition; her interest in animals; the exciting influences of the dance; the dusk of night; the strongly aphrodisiac influence of the flowers; and finally, chance, which brings the pair together in a lonely room, plus the presumption of the excited man',[2] and so on. Strindberg does not realise, or at least does not appear to realise, that many of these motives do not become really discernible in the action. It is true, however, that the existence of a great complexity of factors is brought out through the impulsive, capricious behaviour of Julia, whose dreams and fancies are at times broken by the most clear-sighted contempt both for herself and for Jean.

[1] See above, Chapter II, p. 41.
[2] *S.S.* XXIII, 102.

In the Preface Strindberg describes his conception of the struggle for power, and of the new 'Superman' being evolved by the conflict between the stronger and weaker members of society, a process which Nietzsche had already outlined. He stressed, in a statement in 1894,[1] that he had already found his way to a Superman ideal before reading Nietzsche, and in fact indicated that the Captain in *The Father* was one representative of this new 'scientific' nobility. The Captain, incidentally, is a most un-Nietzschean figure. Strindberg's views on this class struggle as exemplified by *Lady Julia* make a somewhat self-contradictory impression: pity, even regret, for the passing of the old order, is conjured up by the figure of Lady Julia, while the rise of the tough representative of the new ruling class does not, even to Strindberg, really augur a better state of affairs for the future.

Various passages in the Preface, in which the new ideology is expounded, indicate that Strindberg retained a good deal of detachment *vis-à-vis* the two main characters. Perhaps it is this quality, above all, which explains the lasting force of the play. Most Naturalist plays as such have dated rather shockingly; some plays by Gerhart Hauptmann, for instance, have become merely ridiculous. Strindberg's play (which in some respects, it is true, is not truly Naturalist, as it treats a case of an exceptional rather than of an everyday kind) still grips and moves. Strindberg claimed, again in the Preface, to have created 'modern' characters, that is, paradoxically, 'characterless' personages, who cannot be summed up with one epithet, but who, conditioned by the times in which they live, are fluid, complex, indeterminate. One may say that this fact provides

[1] See *Gleanings* (*Efterslåtter*), in *S.S.* LIV, 323.

another reason for the strength of the work, even though the actual moral significance, the tragic finality of the seduction, has dated. I mean by this that human personalities have become more, not less, torn, since Strindberg's play was written, and that, in that sense, the tragedy is still actual.

Two further technical points in this play deserve comment. Strindberg has made skilful use of the setting, midsummer eve, which in Sweden has a peculiar charm of its own, a magic night when the sun does not set, a night which, with the scents and sounds of the brief, intense Northern summer, drives people mad. This midsummer atmosphere is all-pervasive on the stage. The lyrical potentialities of such a night of joy and *längtan* (longing) contrast with the brutality of character and action, and indeed enhance its dramatic effectiveness.

The second point relates to the dialogue. Strindberg has here further developed the technique he followed in *The Father*, in which the conversation seems inconsequent and wandering, but, under cover of this apparent inconsequentiality, makes its points. Strindberg discussed the details of his own technical innovations—or proposed reforms—in the Preface, and also in his later article *Concerning the Modern Drama and the Modern Stage* (*Om Modernt Drama och Modern Teater*), printed in 1889,[1] which provided a theoretical basis for the Naturalist drama.

In *Creditors* Strindberg treats the relations of a woman, Thekla, with her first and second husbands, Gustav and Adolf, respectively. The chief interest of this otherwise dreary play lies in the introduction into it of the power of suggestion. Adolf dies as a result of Gustav suggesting

[1] Published in *S.S.* xvii, 281–303.

to him that he has epilepsy. The struggle, that is to say, to achieve power and deal destruction, is fought between two minds without any visible physical means, another aspect of the problem of suggestion already adumbrated in *The Father* and *Miss Julia*.

6

The group of one-act plays *Pariah* (*Paria*), *The Stronger* (*Den Starkare*), and *Simoom* (*Samum*), which Strindberg composed during the years 1888–9, with the Scandinavian Experimental Theatre in mind, represents a sort of concentration of Naturalist drama. Lasting only a quarter of an hour or less, and requiring not more than three speaking parts (*The Stronger*, in fact, only one), they showed how the technically limited means of production which were at Strindberg's disposal drove him to a *reductio ad absurdum* of Naturalist doctrine. *Pariah* was actually a free adaptation of a story by the writer Ola Hansson,[1] who introduced Strindberg to the works of Edgar Allan Poe, and thereby deepened his already active interest in morbid psychology. Poe continued to influence him for a long time to come; he received his tenebrous stories and mysterious atmosphere with a kind of stormy enthusiasm: 'If you knew', he wrote,[2] 'what I had experienced since I read E.P.—experienced—because I've noticed it.'

As late as 1893 Strindberg produced plays in the Naturalist manner, though by that time he had himself ceased to proclaim his belief in Naturalism as such. Of

---

[1] Ola Hansson, 1860–1925, poet and novelist, one of the first regional writers to celebrate the beauty of Skåne. See also above, Chapter III, pp. 47 f.
[2] Letter to Ola Hansson, from Holte, 2 January 1889.

this group of plays,[1] *The Bond (Bandet)*, 1892, the subject of which is his own divorce and the fate of his children, makes the most powerful impression. The loss of his children also inspired the play *The Keys of Heaven (Himmelrikets Nycklar)*, in which the smith, symbolising Strindberg, goes off in search of his dead children. As in *Lucky Peter's Journey*, the frame is a fairy-story, but much grimmer and more grotesque in character.

Perhaps the most interesting feature of the works of these years is the evidence they afford of the persistence in Strindberg of both realism and symbolism.[2] I mean that the confused and complex current of inspiration, which runs through his works from his youth onwards, defies temporal division. Just as in his most visionary works signs of acute powers of realistic observation are displayed, so the grimly Naturalistic plays often contain, in embryo, elements which point to or resemble the Expressionist[3] grotesqueness of the productions of his later period.

7

In the years of acute spiritual and physical suffering, after Strindberg's divorce and remarriage, which culminated in the so-called Inferno Crisis (see Chapter III), Strindberg wrote very little; but once he had fought his way to a new faith (however shifting in its character),

---

[1] I.e. *Debit and Credit (Debet och Kredit)*, *The First Warning (Första Varningen)*, *Facing Death (Inför Döden)*, *Motherly Love (Moderskärlek)*, and *Playing with Fire (Leka med Elden)*, all 1892.

[2] 'Symbolism may be defined as an attempt by carefully studied means—a complicated association of ideas represented by a medley of metaphors—to communicate unique personal feelings.' (Edmund Wilson, *Axel's Castle*, New York and London, 1947, pp. 21–2.)

[3] Expressionism, a movement in art which endeavours, not to give impressions as such, but to express in the particular art form the state of mind stirred up in the artist by an experience.

his creative energies were enormously stimulated. He turned naturally to the drama again, and his absorption in his own religious conversion first found expression in the two parts of *To Damascus* (*Till Damaskus*), the title of which refers, of course, with characteristically Strindbergian arrogance, to the conversion of St Paul. No doubt the insecure nature of his hold on religion explains the varying forms with which Providence—or God—is endowed in his subsequent works. Sometimes a personal God appears, sometimes blind Chance rules, sometimes again Evil Powers seem to be in control. From the literary point of view, he now especially admired Balzac, his mixture of realism and mysticism, as exemplified in *Séraphita*; and it is worth noting here that he disliked the term 'Symbolist', when it was applied to him now and later, and, when pressed for a definition of his own position, called himself a 'New Naturalist' (Nynaturalist).

It is from his own, almost dreamlike, or, as one may prefer to term it, nightmarish, view of his experiences that *To Damascus* is created, the experiences in question being his second marriage, with Frida Uhl, and the great religious crisis. The second part of the work is built on the same foundation: it was written only six months later, but the tone has become perceptibly harsher. Clearly by dwelling on his own wrongs and disappointments, Strindberg whipped himself up, rather than reconciled himself to his sufferings.

The first part of *To Damascus*—the hero of both parts is the Stranger (den Okände)—turns on the scene in the convent, and the pattern of the structure is built up so that the eight scenes before this focal point and the eight after it correspond in setting. Thus the play opens 'At the Street-corner' (*Vid Gathörnet*), and, having run full circle through its five acts, ends at the same place. The title 'At the Street-corner', incidentally, refers also to the mental state of the Stranger, who, when the curtain rises, stands also at a crossroads in his life. This deliberate technical device helps to create a dream-like atmosphere for the play.

The very simple plot consists in the meeting of the Lady and the Stranger, the Stranger's wooing of her, their elopement, in spite of her husband the Doctor, their subsequent marriage—and discords—and their sufferings together, until the Stranger finds a sort of solution at the end. The Lady is on her way into the church, and urges the Stranger to accompany her, to which entreaty he answers: 'Well, I can always walk through; but I won't stay.' The Lady: 'You don't know. Come. You will hear new songs in there.' The Stranger (following her to the church door): 'Perhaps.' The Lady: 'Come.'[1]

Behind this, at best temporary, reconciliation with the Powers—and the struggle between the Stranger and them forms the inner, the main, conflict of the play— lies a practical fact: the Stranger has found waiting for him at the post office the registered letter containing money, the absence of which has caused him such difficulties and humiliations. The border between the sublime and the ridiculous often becomes narrow indeed in Strindberg's life and works. Yet the character of the Powers, the extent of their might, is never clearly defined; it is even suggested that they, too, are inner experiences, projected by the imagination. In the first scene 'By the Sea' the Stranger challenges them to action: 'Jealous Gods or Devils. Little bourgeois gods who parry the sword's blow with pricks

[1] *S.S.* xxix, 135.

of the needle from behind; who don't come into the field....'[1]

The strength of this play lies, paradoxically, in its vagueness. Its poetry springs from the fact that the incidents are depicted with realistic detail, but at the same time contain an inner meaning. One factor in particular which emphasises the contrast between appearance and reality, and at the same time sharpens the dream-effect is the introduction of 'Doppelgänger', in the sense that many of the characters of the play—and this is suggested rather than stated—are merely other aspects of the Stranger: so for instance the Beggar and the Mad-man. In the convent scene the Stranger is confronted by a number of persons who seem familiar and yet are different (the actual inspiration for the scene Strindberg had received from his own stay in the St Louis Hospital in Paris), and this provokes him to the words: 'But it seems to me I know them all. And I see them as if in a mirror; and they are merely pretending to eat.... Is there some play being produced? There's a couple sitting who are like my parents, but only superficially.'[2] Later, the Confessor introduces him to these beings, against all of whom he has transgressed in some way or other—evidence of the persistent sense of guilt in Strindberg's mind.

The convent scene is the *scène à faire* in *To Damascus*, Part I, if one may use this expression about so unorthodox a play. In Part II, the crux comes in the third act, with the 'Public-House Banquet', as the stage-directions have it. Here a contrast is drawn between the pompous banquet given in the traditional Swedish manner, with an abundance of food, drink, and formal speeches, at which the Stranger, who has discovered the

[1] *S.S.* xxix, 58.   [2] *S.S.* xxix, 91.

secret of making gold, is being hailed as the saviour of mankind, and the dirty, ragged, and sinister figures who line the fourth table when the proceedings start. This grotesque element is further accentuated when the gold vessels are exchanged, in the course of the banquet, for tin mugs, the tables are cleared of the magnificent food, and a screen removed—to reveal a sordid bar and an assemblage of prostitutes and scavengers. The Stranger, abandoned by the respectable guests, finds himself surrounded by this *canaille*, and finally is presented with a bill for the banquet, which he, an alchemist whose pretensions have been exploded, cannot pay. Strindberg, then, with this picture *à la* Toulouse-Lautrec, has found another way of presenting the question: 'What is reality?' It is worth noting how much of the actual setting was suggested to Strindberg by his wanderings round Paris.

Not even at the end of Part II does this supposed narrative of conversion conclude on a positive note. The Stranger's last words, uttered in the same breath as abuse of the Lady and her child—their child—are: 'Come, priest, before I change my mind.'[1]

One cannot really speak of any characterisation in *To Damascus*. The Stranger, portrait of the author himself, provides the link between the subjective and the objective in the shifting scene. The chief interest of the play lies in the technique, the liberation of the drama from its conventional bonds, the use of the setting, which changes, in a sense, with the mood of the character. In *The Dream Play* (*Drömspelet*) Strindberg was to go even further in freeing the drama and giving the contemporary theatre new objectives. *To Damascus* already offers a marked contrast to the close-knit texture of

[1] *S.S.* xxix, 235.

Strindberg's plays of the 'eighties. One must admit that the fluidity and poetry of the later plays are often achieved at the expense of dramatic tension.

8

Advent, written in 1898, and *There are Crimes and Crimes* (*Brott och Brott*), of the following year, both represent steps in Strindberg's attempt to acquire some detachment in his attitude towards those experiences which precipitated and made up the Inferno Crisis. *Advent* Strindberg appears to have planned as a fairy-tale play for children, under the influence of Dickens's Christmas stories and of Hans Andersen; but in the course of writing it he turned it into a mystery play with horror effects. The evil characters in it, the Lawyer and his wife, are so very, very bad, whilst the good characters, that is, the children, seem almost like angels, idealised as they are by Strindberg's longing for his own children. The Devil (den Onde) castigates the wicked, thereby carrying out the intentions of God; but Strindberg goes further than the doctrines of Swedenborg in his vindictiveness. One is reminded of the Queen of Hearts in *Alice in Wonderland* and her cry: 'Off with his head.' *Advent* contains some of Strindberg's crudest supernatural effects and has little permanent value.

There are Crimes and Crimes has its setting in the Paris of Strindberg's own day. It concerns the career of a successful playwright, Maurice, who is threatened with failure. The action revolves round two sets of lovers, Maurice and Jeanne, the good and noble woman, and Adolphe, the artist, and his mistress Henriette, also an artist. She represents that type of woman whom Strindberg so particularly disliked and so persistently returned to, the 'modern' emancipated career woman. Bertha, Thekla, Henriette—their names differ, but their features are alike. Henriette abandons her lover, and with her strong will and ruthless character succeeds in luring Maurice away from Jeanne. The link between the latter and Maurice consists of a child, whom the new lovers wish dead, in fact they will that she shall die. She does die, suddenly; and the question arises: Who killed her? Maurice and Henriette consider themselves guilty, or, rather, consider each other guilty, each torturing the other with suspicions.

Public suspicion fastens on Maurice. As a result of the rumours which arise, his new play is threatened with withdrawal, and he faces complete ruin. Yet, as soon as Maurice, overcome by his feeling of spiritual guilt, has confessed his thoughts to the Abbé, the situation is speedily reversed, with a rapidity which often occurs in Strindberg's plays, and which is perhaps an expression of that curious, almost childlike, volatility of temperament that was peculiar to him. It is proved that the child died from natural causes, Maurice's reputation is cleared, and, when the play ends, he is preparing to return to Jeanne. It all seems rather too pat to convince. The conception of murder by thought links up, of course, with Strindberg's earlier studies of hypnotism in the 'eighties and early 'nineties. The happy ending reflects the improvement in his own spirits. Now exiled, as he termed it, in Lund, he found the surroundings of that little academic backwater dull but soothing.

9

It was in Lund that Strindberg planned the cycle of historical plays, of which, after six months, he had completed the first three (1899), though not in the order which he had originally sketched out. Partly, it was the hope of escaping from his own introspective analysis of the past that drove him to take up the historical drama again; partly, no doubt, the revival of national feeling in Sweden at this time provided a stimulus. The reading and re-reading of Shakespearean plays, the tragedies and the chronicles, was a factor as well as an effect of his interest. He read Swedish chronicle books, Afzelius' *Saga Traditions* (*Sagohäfder*) and Starbäck-Bäckström's *Stories from Swedish History* (*Berättelser ur Svenska Historien*) being his favourite sources, both of them gossipy and anecdotal in character.[1]

From these works Strindberg took what he wanted, and rearranged facts and dates with a sovereign contempt for accuracy; though he professedly wished to escape from the subjective, it is in the light of his own experiences and problems that he looks at history. Naturally, he selects those themes which will illustrate his own ideas, especially the idea that events are arbitrarily decided by Providence, not determined by inflexible laws. As Strindberg later wrote on this topic: 'Everything looks like an enormous game of chess played by a single player, who moves both the black and white pieces.'[2] The heroes of these plays become the mouthpieces of Strindberg's ideas on expiation, but in the sense of being passive victims of vengeance, or agents of an expiation enforced upon them for the sins of their fathers, they lose in tragic grandeur in the Shakespearean sense.

In *The Saga of the Folkungs* (*Folkungasagan*) the hero Magnus sits on the Swedish throne, during the four-

---

[1] He also used Fryxell's *Berättelser ur Svenska Historien*.
[2] See the essay *Världshistoriens Mystik* in *S.S.* LIV, 353.

teenth century, with his son Erik as co-regent. Magnus, in order to avoid further feuds in this already blood-stained family, has deliberately raised his son to the throne; nevertheless the son betrays his father by plotting. According to Strindberg's views, Magnus has challenged fate by acting as he does at the beginning of the play, that is by thanking Heaven for its mercies. There follows a series of disasters: he learns of his wife's unfaithfulness, he suffers defeat in battle, the Black Death appears, and so on. Magnus is presented as the scapegoat who suffers undeservedly. Strindberg indeed depicts him as a benefactor to his people, for he has set free the serfs. It is interesting to see that Strindberg had already moved away from the worship of the Superman, and had reverted to his previously held democratic conception of the Swedish people as the force that mattered, in contradistinction to the King. In this representation of a hero struck down by fate, Strindberg strove to achieve the effect of Greek tragedy, but did not really succeed. Magnus is too querulous for the role. What lends interest to the play is Strindberg's feeling for the pictorial, his crowd scenes, with the bright colours and contrasting shadows of medieval life, the shades and gestures on which he seizes with his quick appreciation of the visually effective. The supernatural element is brought in here, as in *Advent*, but more subtly, as, for instance, in the figure of the 'Plague-Girl' with her vermilion-red face and hands and the broom on her shoulder, who goes round, chalking a cross on the doors of the doomed victims.

Strindberg never completed any other play of the Folkung cycle.[1] Instead, in the spring of 1899, he went

---

[1] With the exception of *The Earl of Bjälbo* (*Bjälbo-Jarlen*). See below, p. 134.

on to *Gustavus Vasa* (*Gustav Vasa*). This furnished him with dramatically more congenial material, in that, as the hero, according to Strindberg's conception, had to be represented as persecuted by fate and expiating, the figure of Gustav Vasa, in its provocativeness, was more suitable for this role. Gustav is a strong king, a forcible personality (both in fact and in Strindberg's play), who is very conscious of what he has accomplished in his country's cause, by freeing Sweden from Danish domination and driving the occupiers out in 1523. Sure of the justice of his cause, he uses his power ruthlessly, to punish any breach of loyalty, to strike down any opposition. Strindberg had already sketched his portrait as a young king in the prose version of *Master Olof*; here he appears as the aging but unbowed and dynamic monarch.

Technically, Strindberg achieves one of his most brilliant feats in the composition of the first two acts, over which the King's presence looms, while he himself remains invisible; a composition probably influenced, as has been pointed out, by Molière's *Tartuffe*. His words echo in those spoken by the other characters. In his strength and ruthlessness he dominates the stage, as Jehovah dominates the Old Testament; and indeed his physical presence, when he does finally appear, reminds one of those Dalecarlian wall-paintings, in which God is depicted with a long white beard, clad in national costume, and sitting like any earthly judge in court.

The first act, particularly, serves to suggest the King's effect on his subjects, and at the same time conveys a good deal of information about the actual situation in the country and the factors that have led up to it. It takes place in Måns Nilsson's house at Aspeboda, near Falun, in the heart of Dalecarlia, the first part of the country to support Gustav in the rising against the

Danes, the first, also, to fight against him. The men of Dalecarlia had helped him to his throne after the massacre at Stockholm,[1] and had again rallied to his assistance, two years before the play opens, when Christian of Denmark had invaded the country by way of Norway.

The King, then, in the opinion of the independent Dalecarlians, owed them a considerable debt of gratitude: Gustav, however, saw no reason for exempting Dalecarlia from the heavy taxes which he must levy in order to settle the national debt to Lübeck. In addition, Gustav decreed that it, like other provinces, should surrender to the Government the church bells and silver vessels in the possession of every parish. Many Dalecarlians, objecting to this 'robbery', opposed the King's agents; some were executed, others left unpunished, and these, in the naïve belief that their existence was essential to the King, thought little of their past offences, and were ready to rebel again. The King, on the other hand, was determined to enforce order throughout the land, and, by settling his debt to Lübeck, to free himself from all dependence on foreign aid. Foreign plots, and the threat of civil war instigated by Dacke and his bands of Småland men, further complicated Gustav's task of reconciling the opposing parties within the country.

Such was the situation, according to Strindberg's version of history, in the year of grace 1533. Its outlines emerge in the conversation between Måns and his wife, and in the ensuing talk between Måns and the other mine-owners who enter the living-room (*Stuga*). The facts slip out naturally in the course of the conversation, which skips from one subject to another, and they are, of course, presented from the point of view of the Dale-

---

[1] *Stockholms Blodbad*, as it was called, took place in 1520, at the instigation of Christian II of Denmark.

carlians. The King has announced that he is coming to Falun: Måns expects him to visit his home on the way, and his friends are to assemble there to meet the King. The atmosphere is heavy with suppressed uneasiness, and, as a result of his wife's repeated warnings, Måns becomes increasingly uncomfortable, and turns gratefully to the distraction provided by his daughter Barbro's entrance. She comes in at the head of a group of little girls, all dressed in mourning, and begins to strew spruce twigs on the floor (this being a Swedish funeral custom), and to sing a special song. These rites Måns has made the children practise, in preparation for their meeting with the King, as a grim reminder to him of Jon of Svärdsjö's death. Jon, one of Gustav's oldest friends in Dalecarlia, had been executed two years before, for sedition against the King. As Måns's anxiety increases, there enter at last Anders Persson, Nils of Söderby, Ingel Hansson, and Master Stig, the pastor. Questions and laconic comments now follow one another in rapid succession. Outwardly all the men appear confident of their own safety, and talk aggressively of the way in which they intend to handle Gustav, relying on a further invasion by Christian of Denmark to complicate the Swedish King's position. A roll of muffled drums interrupts their talk and reminds them of the massacre at Tuna Heath;[1] death is evoked by their memories, by the very scent of the chopped spruce under their feet. Three heavy knocks resound, and there enter, not the King, but his emissaries Olaus Petri and Herman Israel, delegate from Lübeck. Olaus, with a few words, succeeds in making the men feel even more apprehensive, but at

[1] In 1527, on the occasion of a rising among the Dalecarlians, Gustav summoned the rebels to meet him at Tuna, and had some of the leaders executed there.

first pride forbids them to give vent to their fears. The King, thus runs Olaus's message, bids everyone stay at home; those he wishes to see he will summon. So the King's presence, that has made itself felt from the first words of the play, has come even closer. A knock is heard on the door: a messenger has come to summon Ingel Hansson to the King. Ingel goes off defiantly.

During the increasing tension which follows, Olaus cross-questions the others on the state of the province, and provokes them, by his nimbleness of wit, into contradictions and boastings. Another knock sounds. Nils is summoned, and with an affectation of boldness follows the messenger. Nonchalantly Olaus continues his inquisition. Follows a third knock, and a summons for Master Stig. Måns starts to his feet with a cry of 'treachery!' but Olaus checks the outburst with a few harsh words: the combination of severity and dryness is characteristic of this older Master Olof, experienced, shrewd, and tough, so different from the impetuous idealist of Strindberg's early play.

Måns and Anders prowl round the room, as they wait for the outcome. Anders expresses their anguish in the cry: 'In Christ's name, will this never end?' The climax follows immediately: Master Olof opens the doors with the words: 'Yes, this is the end',[1] and the three bloodstained coats of their dead friends are thrown on to the table by the messenger.

The tension snaps, and the two recoil in horror and anger. Master Olof then deals rapidly with them; they will be allowed to go to Stockholm under safe-conduct to see the King. Appealing to Herman Israel as witness, he makes them admit that their grievances had no foundation, and that their own words have confirmed this.

[1] S.S. XXXI, 155.

Whilst Måns and Anders withdraw to an adjoining room to discuss this offer, Olaus and Israel comment on the men of Dalecarlia: 'A very fine people....But rather simple.'[2] These words clearly represent the King's opinion of his 'Dalamän', and, from the technical point of view, explain their role in the play.

The subsequent discussion between Olof and Herman seems based on a flaw, the only flaw, in my opinion, in this act. They are represented as not knowing each other; and, since they both function as emissaries of the King, this seems improbable. The entrance of Barbro and the little girls furnishes another touch of dramatic irony, also of comic relief. They take Israel for the King, and, much to his surprise, kneel before him. The little speech of commendation from Olof gives Strindberg an occasion to stress the *motif* of gratitude, which recurs several times later in the play.

Måns and Anders return, and announce that they will go to Stockholm; clearly, as Olof realises, they remain in a rebellious frame of mind. His last words to them—maintaining the dramatic interest up to the end—tell of the capture of Christian, the Danish king. Thus their final sneaking hope has been dispelled. It must be admitted that this interweaving of themes, and the contrast between the violent *tempo* of the action and the protracted waiting is handled with masterly skill.

In the second act Strindberg, obviously influenced by Shakespeare's method of composition in *Henry IV*, drops the main theme, and introduces a subsidiary one, namely, the relationship between Herman Israel, who plots against Gustav, and his son Jacob, a devoted admirer of the King, and the friendship between Jacob and Gustav's heir, the hysterical Erik. The tavern scene,

[2] *S.S.* xxxi, 159.

wherein Erik and his dissipated companion Göran Persson drink and brawl, is doubtless inspired by Shakespeare. In the moment of attacking Jacob, Erik is arrested by the King's deputy. Erik hates the King, but the very shrillness of his criticism proclaims his dependence on his father. Thus this act, too, serves to emphasise the strength and omnipresence of the King.

When we finally meet the King at the beginning of the third act, it is Gustav as husband and father whom Strindberg first reveals. In the *Open Letters to the Intimate Theatre* (*Öppna Brev till Intima Teatern*) Strindberg wrote many years later: 'Shakespeare's way, in *Julius Caesar*, of depicting historical persons, even heroes, intimately, became the decisive model for my first great historical drama, *Master Olof*, and, with certain reservations, also for those written after 1899.'[1] In *Gustavus Vasa* Strindberg used this approach with great success, without imitating any one Shakespearean hero. Gustav, then, is shown as a loving husband to his wife, and, in his dealings with his son, as a firm, hot-tempered, but wise father. Only after these scenes does he appear as King and diplomat, negotiating with Israel, consulting Olof. He seems doubtful of his right to punish Måns and Anders, who have conspired against him, but, his decision once taken, after almost anguished deliberation, he acts ruthlessly, and condemns the traitors unheard. So far, then, Gustav, threatened by plots, and pressed by foreign creditors, has asserted himself with pride against all dangers. He has pitted his own righteousness and self-confidence against fate, and thus, dramatically speaking, he has challenged fate and paved the way for his own humiliation.

In Act IV the King appears in disguise and mingles

[1] *S.S.* L, 123.

with the beggars in Stockholm, who complain to him about his own acts. Israel, from whom Gustav had hoped for further assistance, has left the country; Dacke, the rebel, is threatening; and Olof urges the King to swallow his pride, and negotiate with the rebel leader. Just as the King, so many years ago, had upbraided Olof for his ruthlessness, so now Olof points out to Gustav all the instances in which he has failed from overweening pride and impetuousness. His frankness enrages but impresses the King, who submits to his advice.

In the last act Gustav has reached the depths of hopelessness. Dacke, backed by the Emperor, has refused to negotiate with the 'perjurer Eriksson', as he calls him, and is marching on Stockholm. In addition, a force of Dalecarlians, presumably also rebels, has encamped on the north side of the town. The King is preparing to flee the country. While the tramp of marching feet is heard —the Dalecarlians marching on the palace—Gustav learns that his last refuge, his ship, has gone aground. As the King stands tense, but finally resigned to his fate, he admits God's justice: it is right that he should be punished. However, his punishment takes an unexpected turn. The tipsy Dalecarlian[1] who climbs cheerfully on to the palace terrace brings another message with him. The Dalecarlians have come to march with the King, not against him, to fight Dacke. The King's last words express his ultimate moral victory over himself: 'O God, Thou hast punished me, and I thank Thee.'[2]

The fourth act is technically the weakest; the fifth, with its grandiose conclusion, compensates for it. It will

---

[1] Strindberg here was certainly influenced by an incident in the play by Frans Hedberg, *Dawn is Breaking* (*Dagen gryr*).

[2] *S.S.* xxxi, 277.

be seen that much of the forcefulness of the work derives from the successful combination of character and action —only too often lacking in Strindberg's plays—by which character provokes incidents, and incidents, in their turn, react upon, and develop, character. Strindberg has succeeded in making of Gustav an attractive figure, in spite of his many shortcomings, suspiciousness, cunning, meanness. Even his enemies, or victims, speak well of him, or, in their abuse, implicitly admit his greatness. In the course of the dialogue Strindberg draws constant comparisons between the King—'God's miracle-man'—and biblical or pagan figures, as a device for making us forget his hero's faults.

In the breadth of canvas, which forms one of the chief merits of *Gustavus Vasa*, Strindberg certainly had Shakespeare as his master. Richness of texture, and variety of character-drawing, one must also allow the work. A further strength lies in the prose, which is simple, eloquent, and extraordinarily varied, never affectedly archaic, but catching at the same time the rhythms of sixteenth-century Swedish.

Gustavus Vasa is far and away the most successful of Strindberg's later historical plays, though not the typical one. In *Erik XIV*, the next, the composition has already become much more episodic. The character of Erik Strindberg had already sketched in the preceding drama: the 'characterless', tormented, and poetical prince bears many resemblances to the author, and this portrait and that of Göran Persson, make the work interesting rather than satisfactory.

These three dramas (*The Saga of the Folkungs, Gustavus Vasa* and *Erik XIV*) proved popular successes. Strindberg's subsequent attempts in this *genre* provoked increasingly sharp criticism at home for their nonchalant treatment of historical facts, and the use of modern, slangy, language, of which *Erik XIV* already offers examples.

Gustavus Adolphus (Gustav Adolf), composed in 1899, and *Engelbrekt* and *Charles XII (Carl XII)*, both of 1901, are already much weaker. *Gustavus Adolphus*, of all Strindberg's efforts the most ambitious in scope, dealing as it does with the tangled skein of the Thirty Years' War, contains some fine scenes. Gustav, like Magnus, like Strindberg, becomes the blind instrument of the 'Powers'. By the time Strindberg composed *Engelbrekt* and *Charles XII*, his belief in expiation had already lost its hold on him, and these later plays, therefore, lack unity of inspiration. They are either more and more episodic, or else colourlessly conventional, like, for instance, *Engelbrekt*, the latter a result of Strindberg's efforts to ward off the unfavourable criticism he had received, which barred the way to production. The most marked tendency is to peg the incidents on to the titular figure, as in *Christina (Kristina)* or *Charles XII*, in which the hero takes on a very different personality from that ascribed to him by the Swedish Romantics or Neo-Romantics. The enigmatic, fatalistic Charles is surrounded by Maeterlinckian symbols and shadows; even the curious crowd scenes strike one as dreams rather than reality. *Gustav III* (1902) conforms more slickly to the type of French drama *à la* Scribe. In *The Nightingale of Wittenberg (Näktergalen i Wittenberg)* Strindberg took up a European, as opposed to a Swedish, theme, that is, the mission of Martin Luther, and depicted the background of the Reformation. The play strikes one as an unsuccessful and coarser version of *Master Olof*.

Several years later (in 1908) Strindberg produced yet another group of historical plays: *The Last Knight (Den*

Siste Riddaren), *The Regent* (*Riksföreståndaren*) and *The Earl of Bjälbo* (*Bjälbo-Jarlen*). It cannot be said that he accomplished anything new or aesthetically perfect in these plays of his old age; it is, however, understandable that, as he had scored his greatest successes abroad with the *genre* of historical drama, he should continue to press the wine out of the grapes. It is to be observed that the immediate occasion for composing these last historical plays was the approach of his sixtieth birthday in January 1909. Finally it should be said, too, that the dimness of these works should not be allowed to obscure his brilliant contributions in this field of drama.

10

Strindberg's renewed creative activity, which had first led him to embark on the historical cycle, took other forms as well. *Easter* (*Påsk*) and *Caspar's Shrove Tuesday* (*Kaspers Fet-tisdag*) were also written in 1900, *Midsummer* (*Midsommar*) and *The Dance of Death* (*Dödsdansen*) in 1901. It is unnecessary to dwell on the trivialities of *Caspar* and *Midsummer*, but *Easter* should be mentioned for the portrait of the young girl Eleonora, whose half-crazed, visionary utterances attain to a certain poetic level. Sanctimonious almost beyond belief is Strindberg's tone in this story of Swedish bourgeois life at its dreariest.

One could hardly find a more striking contrast to *Easter* than *The Dance of Death*, a dissection in Strindberg's expert manner of the 'eighties of the love-hate relationship between man and woman. The apparently ceaseless tormenting of each other by the Captain and Alice, his wife, becomes to Strindberg a symbol of life itself. The first part ends on the note of death bringing release: 'Perhaps, when death comes, life will begin',[1] says the Captain after his stroke. In the second part the Captain suffers another and fatal stroke, and in grotesque triumph Alice has his corpse carried out; then she begins to recall her dead husband as he had been in his youth, and to think of him in a forgiving spirit. It is to be noted that here, on the whole, Strindberg, contrary to his usual practice, condemns the man rather than the woman. *The Dance of Death* provides further evidence of what has already been indicated above, the co-existence in Strindberg's work, at one and the same time, of various literary manners.

Curiously enough, Strindberg introduces a lyrical *motif* into the embittered domesticity of *The Dance of Death*, with the relationship between Judith, the young daughter, and Allan: this reflects the new emotional influence at work in his own life, introduced by his meeting with Harriet Bosse. The same influence explains the volume he published in 1902, containing *The Crown Bride* (*Kronbruden*), *Swan-white* (*Svanevit*) and *The Dream Play* (*Drömspelet*), the last being much the most fascinating of the three. In *The Crown Bride* Strindberg takes up the folk-tale *motif* of the unmarried mother who murders her child, and clothes it in rather mannered but effectively laconic language. *Swan-white*, based on fairy-tale and folk-song, owes its inspiration, as Strindberg himself admitted, to Maeterlinck, whose plays he had read as early as the 'nineties, but whose decisive influence upon him was brought to bear through his reading of the collection of essays entitled *Le Trésor des Humbles*, in 1901. Strindberg was interested in Maeterlinck's ideas rather than in his plays, admired his spirituality, but was intrigued also by his conception of 'the tragedy of

[1] *S.S.* XXXIV, 121.

everyday', that is, the scenes of everyday life behind which the 'Powers' are at work, the Powers in which Strindberg also believed. For Maeterlinck, silences become as expressive as words, or even more expressive; hence the heavy pauses and the long-drawn-out exclamations of his dialogue. Strindberg, at first, probably exaggerated his affinities with the rarefied Maeterlinck; it should be noted that he claimed to have independently anticipated some of the Belgian's ideas in his own use of dialogue, and so on, but it seems fairly certain that Maeterlinck's influence can be discerned in some of the plays after 1901—at its least felicitous in *Swan-white*, where the naïve babblings of the Princess almost parody Maeterlinck's heroines.

The scraps of sketches, jottings, and unfinished manuscripts which Strindberg carried round with him in his lifetime in the bag known as *gröna säcken* (the green bag) indicate how important a part visual inspiration played in his method of dramatic construction, particularly after the Inferno Crisis. This visual method of conception can be followed in the surviving drafts of *The Dream Play*, which first bore the title *Waiting* (*Väntan*), then *The Growing Castle* (*Det Växande Slottet*). Here the original core of the play was the scene in the passage outside the Opera House, where the officer paces backwards and forwards with a bouquet in his hand, waiting for Victoria, the singer. So had Strindberg, in his youth, waited for Siri von Essen outside Dramaten; and so he paced, almost forty years later, as he waited for Harriet Bosse after her performance. The portress sits on the left of the gate into the passage, crocheting a quilt in star pattern; she has been working on it for the last twenty-six years. The bill-sticker is washing down the wall, in preparation for putting up the new posters for the Opera; by his side, leaning against the wall, stands the fishing-net with a green handle, which he has at last acquired after years and years of expectation. A frail lime-tree is just bursting into leaf; on the right stands a door with a clover-leaf-shaped airhole.

From this basic framework many of the transformations of the scenery spring. Thus, when the scene changes to the lawyer's office, the portress's lodge has become the lawyer's writing alcove, the tree, now denuded of leaves, serves as a hatstand, and the mysterious door has become part of a cupboard for documents; the gate is a doorway in the railing which runs across the stage. In the church scene the railing recurs as the chancel rail; the lawyer's notice-board now indicates the numbers of the hymns, the linden hatstand becomes a candelabrum, and the four-leaved-clover door now leads to the vestry. Just before the end the original passage reappears, and the door, the mysterious door, is at last opened, to reveal—nothing. Everything temporal, Strindberg tells us, is hollowness and mockery, 'Vanity of vanities, all is vanity, saith the preacher'.

At the very end, the backcloth of the castle, showing a gilded roof 'with a crown-shaped flower-bud at the top'.[1] which was displayed at the beginning, is lowered again. Now, on the roof of the castle, the chrysanthemum bud is seen, on the point of bursting into flower. The castle symbolises the place of origin of the god Indra's daughter, who has descended to earth, and, in the form of Agnes, has endured the lot of a mortal. To this castle she now returns, to carry back to the gods, as she has promised, the prayers of men. As she enters, the castle rises in flames, the chrysanthemum flowers, and, as the stage directions have it, the light illumines 'a wall

[1] *S.S.* xxxvi, 221.

of human faces, questioning, sorrowing, despairing'.[1]
The actual visual experience behind this dream of the
castle—and the evidence casts interesting light on
Strindberg's creative processes—was the view of the
barracks called Hästgårdskasernen, in Sturevägen (now
Lidingövägen), Stockholm. The black roof of this
building is topped by a golden crown; the building was
one which Strindberg particularly admired, and he
refers to it in other works.

In *The Dream Play*, Indra's daughter moves through
these shifting scenes and others, experiencing the joys,
but above all the sorrows, of a mortal, in company with
her husband the lawyer, the officer, the poet, all different manifestations of the same person, who is Strindberg, and again is not. The Author's Note at the beginning states that the writer 'has tried to imitate the dis-
jointed but apparently logical form of a dream. Anything may happen: everything is possible and probable.
Time and space do not exist.... The characters are
split, doubled, and multiplied: they evaporate and are
condensed, are diffused and concentrated. But a single
consciousness holds sway over them all—that of the
dreamer.'[2] Yet the play appears to contradict this.
Rather, it is the whole of this earthly life which Strindberg considers a dream, and which arouses his pity.
'Men are to be pitied'[3] becomes the theme of his message of resignation before the trials of mankind. To the
problem of what is reality, which had been taken up in
To Damascus, Strindberg persistently returns. Some
lines from the conversation between the Daughter and
the Poet, in Fingal's Cave, express his idea. The

[1] *S.S.* xxxvi, 330.
[2] *S.S.* xxxvi, 215.
[3] Cf. Maeterlinck's *Pelléas et Mélisande*, Act IV, Scene ii, Arkel's words:
'Si j'étais Dieu, j'aurais pitié du cœur des hommes.'

Daughter: 'All these I have dreamt.' Poet: 'I made a poem of them all.' Daughter: 'Thou knowest then what poetry is.' Poet: 'No, I know what dreaming is.... What is poetry?' Daughter: 'Not reality, but more than reality...not dreaming, but waking dreams.'[1] Here is Strindberg at his most visionary.

Yet *The Dream Play* also contains details of the crudest realism; in the lawyer's cramped home the air reeks of cabbage, and the baby cries. The second half of the work tends to drag a little, but nevertheless, with it, Strindberg has advanced another step towards the liberation of the drama from conventional restraints. The Prologue, added before the first production in 1907, again sounds a harsher note. In it Strindberg once more fulminates against humanity.

To Damascus III was not published till 1904, but much of it was composed as early as 1900, with the scenes about his third marriage inserted later. As a whole, it expresses the resigned pessimism which colours *The Dream Play*; this pessimism culminates in the decision of the Stranger to retire to a non-denominational monastery—a refuge of loneliness—after balancing the accounts of his three marriages.

I I

Much the most valuable aspect of Strindberg's later work, that is, in the period between 1902 and his death in 1912, is crystallised in the *Chamber Plays* (*Kammarspel*), which, published in 1907 (except for *The Black Glove* (*Svarta Handsken*)), were composed for production at the 'Intimate Theatre' (Intima Teatern), the great venture of Strindberg's old age.

[1] *S.S.* xxxvi, 301.

In his already mentioned *Open Letters to the Intimate Theatre*, Strindberg defined the term 'Kammarspel', with reference to Reinhardt's 'Kammarspielhaus' in Berlin, as 'the idea of chamber music transferred to the drama. The intimate procedure, the significant motif, the careful treatment.'[1] *The Storm* (*Oväder*), the first of the group, approximates, perhaps, most closely to this definition. Its simple theme presents as hero an aging man, alone in his flat in a big apartment house in Stockholm, during the summer when the town is deserted. Sitting alone during the long summer evenings, he lives with his memories of wife and daughter who have left him, just like Strindberg himself after Harriet Bosse and Anne-Marie had gone away. He discovers, in the course of the play, that his former wife and her second husband have just moved into the flat above, and he and his wife meet again after five years' absence from each other. In the third and last act, the father fears that his daughter has been kidnapped, but he hears before the end that she is safe. The last act, like the first, plays outside the flat in the twilight; the storm which gives the work its title has passed over, just as has the disturbance which threatened the hero's peace of mind; and, as the curtain falls, the lamplighter appears —autumn is on the way. Of all Strindberg's works, *The Storm* is the most subdued and discreet in treatment, with an atmosphere of wistful charm, which does recall Maeterlinck's works, especially *Intérieur*, but which is, at least partially, explained by the personal mood underlying it; Strindberg's own feeling of withdrawal from the world into his happy memories, as he expressed it in letters to Harriet Bosse. This makes *The Storm*, with its evocation of the long, silent, summer evenings in Stockholm, and of

[1] *S.S.* L, II.

the old man's longing for solitude, and at the same time his dread of it, one of the most moving of Strindberg's plays.

In *After the Fire* (*Brända Tomten*) Strindberg chooses the theme of a stranger returning to his old home and finding it burnt down, with all the ruins exposed to the gaze of the passers-by; all the old memories and scandals are exposed too. Under the penetrating eye of the Stranger the old feuds and injustices are dragged out into the daylight. It is discovered that the fire was started by arson, and the Stranger departs, after leaving the wreath he had brought for his parents' grave on the débris of the house as a symbol of mourning for his lost illusions. Strindberg succeeded in making the presence of the tenement house—incidentally, it is his own old home in Norrtullsgatan—tangible; but otherwise the play shocks by its self-righteous bitterness, and lacks the compensation provided by the fantastic.

The fantastic element, however, looms very large in *The Ghost Sonata* (*Spöksonaten*), in which the hero, a young student, being 'Sunday's child', has second sight. The play thus opens with a curious *rencontre* between this student and a milkmaid at a street pump, the milkmaid being really an apparition, invisible to the eyes of the old man Hummel, who has decided to make himself the patron of the gallant young man. The student is initiated by Hummel, a sinister figure in a wheel-chair, into the fortunes of the various families inhabiting the prosperous-looking mansion in Östermalm, and is introduced to the Young Lady (Fröken), the Colonel's daughter, whom he has admired at a distance. She is delicate, fading away from life. All the families are represented at the gathering convened according to custom by the Colonel, 'Spöksupén', as the footman describes it: 'The usual ghost supper, as we call it. They drink tea, don't say a single word, or else the Colonel does all the talking.... They look like ghosts and they have kept this up for twenty years, always the same people, saying the same things, or saying nothing at all for fear of being found out.'[1] And in answer to the other servant's question about the Colonel's wife, the footman comments: 'Oh yes, but she's a little cracked; she sits in a cupboard, because her eyes cannot bear the light.'[2] This, then, is the happy circle to which the student is anxious to gain access.

At the ghost supper, when it does take place, the old man sets out to expose all the guests in turn, having first privately unmasked the Colonel. The Young Lady is his daughter, not the Colonel's, and Hummel's intrigues aim at making a match between the student and the sick daughter, in the hope of saving her life. But Hummel in his turn is exposed by the Mummy, who has sat for twenty years in her closet, and during that time has prattled like a parrot, but now speaks out clearly. So he, too, becomes a sort of parrot, repeats his senseless cries, and retires behind the screen to die. Meanwhile the Student, who, in his path towards winning the girl, has seen so many of his beliefs shattered, while he still loves her, cannot (just like Strindberg) refrain from telling her the truth as he sees it, that is, that she is incapable of really living life. Withered by the harsh breath of truth, she dies, in the midst of the hyacinths which she has cherished, and the Student greets death as her liberator, in a curious but poetical little invocation to Buddha, which, like the mythology introduced into *The Dream Play*, reminds us that Strindberg dabbled in Buddhist philosophy.

[1] *S.S.* XLV, 174, 175.   [2] *S.S.* XLV, 175.

There is, then, some attempt at reconciliation, and harmony follows on the extraordinarily bitter and grotesque exposure of all illusions, which is the theme of *The Ghost Sonata*. In many or most of Strindberg's plays one character has the faculty of seeing through everything; here it seems as though everything were seen through by everyone. In the words of the Colonel, as quoted by the Young Lady: 'What is the use of talking, when you can't impose upon each other?'[1] Even Strindberg could go no further along these lines. *The Ghost Sonata* offers plentiful evidence of the exuberance of Strindberg's imagination, especially in the grotesque element, bordering on the comic, indeed often going over the edge; the episode with the gigantic, sinister, grinning Cook may be cited as a good instance of this. With *The Ghost Sonata*, Strindberg really created a new kind of symbolism.

The *Pelican* (*Pelikanen*) is a more realistic play, but degenerates into a grotesque exaggeration of realism, and provides an opportunity for Strindberg to return to his King Charles's Head, the wicked unscrupulous selfishness of woman. *The Black Glove*, the last of the *Chamber Plays*, reverts to the Dickensian Christmas themes of Strindberg's youth and middle age. It is a Christmas story, containing some fine passages, but not, technically, reaching a high level, nor expressing anything new.

Not till 1909 did Strindberg take his farewell of the stage, in *The Great Highway* (*Stora Landsvägen*), where the sixty-year-old writer, in a kind of continuation of *To Damascus*, looks back upon his past life. The sub-title, 'a drama of wandering, with seven stations', with its allusion to Christ's Passion, underlines the connection with the earlier work. Strindberg himself appears in the

[1] *S.S.* LXV, 199.

role of the Hunter who comes down from the mountains, treads the weary and dusty way among human beings, and at the end resolves to flee back to the Alps and a snowy grave. No dramatic conflict, no plot of any kind, interrupts what is really a lyrical monologue, or, at most, dialogue. In this reckoning of accounts with himself and with life, Strindberg continues to voice the bitterest reproaches for the wrongs he has (in his own opinion) so unjustly suffered. In the last few lines of the very beautiful final soliloquy his own agonised regret rings out: 'I first who have suffered most, who have suffered most from the pain of not being able to be the person I wished to be'[1]—yet, even to the last, arrogance mingles with the sorrow.

Strindberg, then, unlike Goethe in *Faust*, never, in all his plays, attained to a philosophic and aesthetic detachment in respect of his experience of life; and his works are the poorer for it. As one looks back on the long—too long—list of his dramas (and space has forbidden the mention here of various uncompleted projects and fragments), certain general characteristics stand out. One is this obsessional absorption in his own sufferings which so often limits, where it does not destroy, his power of character-drawing. Most dramatists portray themselves, at one time or another, in some chosen character or characters; in Strindberg's work the hero only too often appears as a caricature of his creator.

Connected with the constant analysis of his own experience is Strindberg's restless desire to explain, to the world and himself, but primarily to himself, the reasons underlying the experience, and the causes conditioning the character. His own modifications of view were marked by the rapidity of his changes in emotion and

[1] *S.S.* LI, 99.

mood, so that often he conceives a drama under the influence of one belief, and, before he has finished it (and his speed of writing hardly requires any further emphasis), has moved on to another point of view. All this makes for inconsistency, but reveals also an enormous, almost animal, vitality, which somehow carries him over his own morbid vulnerability, another aspect of the dualism which he reveals. Thus his plays provide a catharsis for himself, rather than for the audience. Even his sense of humour, paradoxically enough, at times, but only at times, proves a source of strength to him. Boldness in conception he never lacks, nor the gift of language, and his most grotesque creations can take on the relief and the rich colouring of a Rouault masterpiece. There were occasions when he himself realised where lay his greatest gift. A letter to his German translator, Emil Schering,[1] sums up his contribution to the European drama: 'Wir haben hundert Dramen zu machen. Aber ich muss dabei sein, und entwerfen, denn das ist meine Stärke.'[2]

[1] Dated 6 May 1907.
[2] 'We have a hundred dramas to create. But I must participate, and sketch them out, for in that lies my strength.'

CHAPTER VI

THE NOVELS

I

JUST as the appearance of the prose version of *Master Olof* marked the beginning of a new epoch in the Swedish theatre, so the publication of *The Red Room* (*Röda Rummet*) in 1879 started an entirely new phase in the development of the Swedish novel. The significance of *Master Olof* was only retrospectively recognised by the Swedes; *The Red Room*, however, immediately attracted a great deal of attention and provoked much discussion, in fact, it provided Strindberg with his first taste of literary success.

The Swedish novel, like the Swedish drama, had suffered from the lack of economic and social stimulus, and had developed late. Such native works as were composed in the seventeenth century were imitations of the pastoral novel, or adaptations of Icelandic sagas, scarcely deserving to be called original compositions, or indeed novels. The first real, original novel in Swedish, by Mörk and Törngren, *Adalrik and Giöthilde* (*Adalrik och Giöthilda*), appeared as late as 1742-4, and that too, though modelled on the work of Mademoiselle de Scudéry and Fénelon, was set against an Icelandic background. The interest it had for contemporaries derived partly from its being a *roman à clé*, and the veiled allusions it contains to politics and personalities appear to form its only links with realistic narrative.

Both in this work and in Mörk's later and more mature novel *Thekla*, the handling of the psychology

leaves much to be desired, and, though the writing of
prose narrative as such made progress during the eighteenth century, this lack of psychological understanding,
or, rather, the lack of any interest in psychology, must,
in part at any rate, explain the absence of any authentic
novels during that century. It is true that in the eighteenth century a certain knowledge of French philosophy filtered into Sweden, and French and English
novels, both in the original and in translation, came to
form a part of the popular reading matter of the time;
but the curious fact is, that this kind of novel-reading
appears at first to have affected comparatively un-
educated, rather than literary, circles. At the end of the
century translations of German sentimental novels, such
as those by Kotzebue, and of Lafontaine, enjoyed a
special vogue, and on these, as well as on the less literary
'robber-romances', the rising generation of Romantic
writers was nurtured.

Not until the first decade of the nineteenth century
did the first true novel of satirical observation of contemporary society make its appearance, with *Uno von
Trasenberg*, by Fredrik Cederborgh. In this book the
Stockholm of 1810 is depicted with a gay and lively
irony: the gambling hells, the secret societies, the
government offices, to which last Strindberg was to
return in *The Red Room*. Unfortunately *Uno von Trasenberg* had no successors of its kind: the Romantic writers
followed other ideals, but achieved, in the *genre* of the
novel, as little as they did in the drama. Almquist, in
some respects a Romantic, in other respects standing
apart from the Romantic movement, provided the only
considerable exception to this statement, for instance
with *The Queen's Jewel (Drottningens Juvelsmycke)*; but the
very power of the fantastic element, and the very

originality of his writing worked against, rather than for, the strengthening of a tradition. Almquist, perhaps, actually did more for the *novell* than for the novel proper, especially with his stories of peasant life; and his tale *That's all right* (*Det går an*), in which he championed love outside marriage (and incidentally finally discredited himself in his clerical profession), was the boldest piece of realistic social criticism before Strindberg. There followed, as in other countries, but more feebly than in most, a crop of historical novels *à la* Walter Scott (Almquist himself sinned in this respect), and in the 1840's came a number of mystery stories, inspired by such foreign models as those of Eugène Sue; among these August Blanche's stories about Stockholm life were especially popular, and so were Almquist's pot-boilers.

Curiously enough, as in England, most of the initial work in developing the novel as a picture of society and a vehicle for ideas was accomplished by certain women writers in the 1830's and 1840's, by Frederika Bremer, Sofia von Knorring, and Emilie Flygare-Carlén, none of whom, unfortunately, rose to anywhere near the genius of a Brontë or an Austen, but all of whom were at least capable of observing and analysing human behaviour, on however limited a canvas, and of raising certain problems for debate. Of these three, the least aesthetically satisfying, Emilie Flygare-Carlén, had, in some ways, the widest range of scene: she did some of her best work in stories about the fishermen and pietists of Western Sweden. Unfortunately, even her best work is marred, as is so much of her sister novelists', by sentimentality and over-ingenuity of plot.

It was the achievement of Viktor Rydberg, novelist, poet and popular philosopher of the 'fifties, to project his ideas on Hellenic paganism into a novel, *The last Athenian (Den siste Athenaren)*, 1859, which skilfully depicts the background of Athens in A.D. 350, the clash of Christian and Pagan personalities, and the plot connecting them, and yet also presents Rydberg's criticism, from his liberal standpoint, of certain aspects of contemporary Swedish culture, in particular of the Swedish Lutheran Church. Rydberg wrote other novels in which ideology is of more interest than the treatment of psychology; in fact, as a novelist, he was too philosophical to exercise an immediate or strong, vitalising influence on the *genre*.

We have already seen that the 'sixties and 'seventies formed a period of sterility in the Swedish drama, till Strindberg's coming. The observation applies equally to other branches of Swedish literature and thought at this time, when the anaemically refined, idealistic 'Pseudonym poets' ('Signaturskalderna'), encouraged by Dietrichson, set the tone, wrote careful, charming, but colourless verses, and Wirsén, their leader, in fact disapproved even of the high-minded Rydberg. Among this mediocrity, an honourable exception must be made for the poetry of Snoilsky, who, however, for many reasons, not least his aristocratic birth, stands apart from the main current of Swedish letters.

This abbreviated account is inserted in order to show how little Swedish literature, at the time of Strindberg's *début* in fiction, was in touch with the world around it, how little adapted to the expression of new thoughts and points of view, which, in fact, were meanwhile being introduced from the Continent by the translations of French and English works, old and new, such as Tocqueville's *La Démocratie en Amérique*, Darwin's *Origin of Species*, and Buckle's *History of Civilisation in England*.

Increased contacts with Norway and Denmark, where the tendency to realism, fostered by political and social dissatisfaction, had already found expression both in theory and practice, in Brandes's articles, and in Ibsen's and Bjørnson's plays, further prepared the soil in Sweden. Yet backward Sweden still remained. In 1866 the long-postponed and much-debated liberal reform of the constitution had been carried through, and, though the results of this, in the form of a gradual democratisation of all aspects of life, were making themselves felt in the 'seventies, no obviously progressive measures were initiated by the new Parliament. The new members, many of them peasants, evinced a markedly conservative tendency, and whilst, temporarily at least, the country made striking progress in the economic sphere, in other fields there was stagnation. The Lutheran Church continued to be the dominant spiritual power, and maintained a close control over intellectual matters, not least in the Universities, in spite of increasing opposition from Pietistic circles (*läsarne*). Rydberg's book *The Bible's Doctrine concerning Christ* (*Bibelns Lära om Kristus*), which appeared in 1862, did more, perhaps, than any other single work in Sweden to popularise a critical approach to Christian orthodoxy, stirring up, needless to say, severe disapproval of work and author in Church circles.

It can thus be seen that in Sweden there was no time for a slow assimilation of the recent scientific discoveries and the new scientific ideas, which, in France and England, were themselves the product of a growing spirit of enquiry, applied, little by little, to every sphere of life and thought; that is, in Sweden acquaintance was not gradually made with modern materialist philosophy, before this philosophy was expressed in the works of foreign writers of *belles lettres*, as for instance in the novels of Zola.[1] The Swedish works inspired by these new and corrosive ideas followed close on the foreign models themselves. No doubt the suddenness of the eruption partially explains the violence of the opposition provoked, for example, by Strindberg's writings. For whilst *The Red Room*, as I have said, attracted attention, its success was also that of a *succès de scandale*.

2

Strindberg had no experience of novel-writing before *The Red Room*.[2] The collected sketches printed under the title *Town and Gown*[3] (*Från Fjärdingen och Svartbäcken*) in 1877, should, technically speaking, be considered rather in the immediately following chapter, with the short stories; but it is, on other grounds, more useful to deal with them here, in that they, in a fragmentary and rudimentary form, contain something of the technique Strindberg was to employ in *The Red Room*. They are sketches of life in Uppsala, as Strindberg had observed and loathed it, during his own periods of sojourn there. In Sweden, as in most other Continental countries at this time, and especially in those under German influence, the student was a popular and glamourised figure, in both life and letters. In England, even allowing for certain glorified fictional accounts of undergraduate life at Oxford and Cambridge, the student, as a social figure, has never enjoyed the kind of false romantic charm

---

[1] E.g. *Les Rougon-Macquart*, 1871–93.
[2] The novel projected sometime between 1871 and 1874, and published for the first time in 1948 with the title *A Story from Stockholm's Skerries* (*En Berättelse från Stockholms Skärgård*) remained a fragment.
[3] See above, Chapter II, p. 30.

which surrounded the feckless, punch-drinking young—
and middle-aged—students of Uppsala.

After his own struggles to exist in that University
town, Strindberg retained no illusions as to the romantic charm of life there, and his sketches, or stories, whilst
good-humoured in tone, were designed to 'debunk' the
cherished ideals of academic life. For instance, *The Victim (Offret)* describes the wretched young man who is too
poor to take part in student life, because he has refused
to accept any financial support from his father, who was
willing to give such support only on the unacceptable
condition that the son should become ordained. In the
end the young man gives way, and becomes a clergyman without vocation, spiritually 'dead'. In *Primus
and Ultimus (Primus och Ultimus)* Strindberg contrasts the
brilliant and wealthy, aristocratic humanist, who appears to have every success before him, but goes mad,
with the poor scientist, who determines to make the best
of life, enters a factory as a chemist, and works his way
up. In the last sketch of the series, *The Old and the New
(Det Gamla och det Nya)*, the most significant of them all,
Strindberg shows up the lazy, sentimental attitude to
life of the superannuated idealist, follower of Boström's[1]
philosophy, and contrasts with this the realistic young
man of his own generation, in fact himself. 'You call us
blasé, because we are hard-working and sensible; believe
me, our feelings are much fresher where they lie, hermetically sealed, than yours that are for show, shop-
worn, and fly-blown.'[2] Through these sketches of real
persons, whom Strindberg had himself known, Uppsala

[1] Christopher Boström (born 1797, died 1866) held the chair of practical philosophy in Uppsala from 1842 to 1863. As Sweden's chief philosopher, he exercised a very considerable influence on academic youth,
long after his death.
[2] *S.S.* III, 106–7.

with its narrow streets and stuffy lecture-rooms is conjured up, vividly, but not nearly so vividly as Stockholm in *The Red Room*.

The Red Room takes its title from the name of the room at Bern's café in Stockholm, meeting-place of the journalists, artists, and poor intellectuals who made up Strindberg's own coterie, especially in the years 1872–4, but also later. Many of the portraits in the book are modelled on actual members of the circle, though naturally modified, for reasons of discretion; others are composite creations; but the book, as a whole, draws its strength and impetus from the fact that Strindberg was writing from his own experiences, as free-lance journalist, temporary civil servant, unsuccessful author, and member of this penurious Bohemian clique, who, sitting on the red plush sofas of Bern's, dissected life and politics over glasses of punch, and found them both *Bosch* (rubbish).

The link, in a sense, between this nucleus and the other spheres of Stockholm life which are depicted in the novel, is Arvid Falk, brother of Grosshandlare (big business man) Carl Nicolaus Falk. Arvid Falk, when the book opens, has just dismissed himself from his post as temporary civil servant in the Department for the Paying Out of Civil Servants' Salaries, after he had earlier left the five other departments to which he had belonged, for the same reason, namely that the work was nominal only. This fact, while not deterring large numbers of other civil servants attached to the various government departments (and so enjoying a position and a title), offended Arvid Falk's sense of honesty. Arvid, in fact, is an idealist, a poet, who has decided to fight for his living as a journalist and writer, and, accordingly, to renounce his social position as *häradshövding* (barrister-

153

at-law). His revelations concerning the Civil Service are naïvely poured out to Struve, the exceedingly venal reporter, in the opening scene of the book, and Struve, ready as always to make trouble for others, later writes them up in an article for a sensational rag, *The People's Banner*, and lets it get round that Falk is the author—an incident comparatively insignificant in itself, but symptomatic of the corruption and treachery against which Arvid comes up all the time. And yet Arvid is not at all deficient in critical intelligence and sense of irony, as his comments to Struve indicate. See, for example, his description of the routine of the Payment Department, where he is being conducted round by a porter: 'At last we stopped outside a door on which was written in letters of gold: "The President." I wanted to open the door and step in, but was respectfully prevented by the porter, who, with real anxiety, took hold of my arm and whispered "Ssssh". "Is he sleeping?" I could not refrain from asking. "For Heaven's sake, don't say anything; nobody can come in here till the President rings." "Does the President often ring, then?" "Oh no, I haven't heard him ring during all the years I've been here."'[1]

Idealist as Falk is, he is doomed to have a hard time in his struggle for a livelihood, which takes him through various newspaper offices, the Conservative *Gråkappan* (*The Grey Coat*), really the *Nya Dagligt Allehanda*, *Rödluvan* (*The Red Cap*), a hit by Strindberg at *Dagens Nyheter*, then to the publishing firm controlled by the Jewish capitalist Smith, who specialises in religious publications, and to the meetings of the dud Insurance Company 'Triton', not to mention the proceedings of the Swedish Parliament, which he also attends as reporter.

[1] *S.S.* v, 13–14.

'The chief clerk reads out a request or resolution concerning the granting of funds for new rope mats for the hall, and brass number-plates on the shelves for over-boots. The motion is passed: "Where does the Opposition sit?" asks the uninitiated (Falk). "The devil only knows. But they say yes to everything." ' [1] Strindberg draws a critical picture of all political parties; when the impartial and honest man gets up to speak for the oppressed, he is ignored by everybody, and members and reporters alike disappear in search of food.

By means of Arvid Falk's experiences, his contacts with his brother Carl Nicolaus's dubious financial affairs, the descriptions of the latter's (and his wife's) vulgarly ostentatious display of wealth, Mrs Falk's participation in the philanthropic venture, *Barnkrubban Bethlehem* (Bethlehem Day Nursery), under the guidance of the fashionable Pastor Skåre, and all the adventures of the Bohemian coterie which has already been mentioned, Strindberg gives a cross-section of life in the capital—a satiric, grotesque, but vivid evocation of the Stockholm of the 1870's, indeed with glimpses of provincial life as well, for certain of the characters are transplanted, in the course of the story, to the provinces.

Life in Bohemian circles as represented in fiction before Strindberg's day had often been endowed with a false glamour. The curious assembly of artists and intellectuals who doss down in Lill-Jans or Vita Bergen and drink in the Red Room, when one or other of them can raise some cash, are not intended to be romantic figures. Strindberg had begun his debunking of the contemporary scene in *Town and Gown*, in a mild way; in *The Red Room* he already manifests much greater confidence and writes with much more verve, when

[1] *S.S.* v, 115.

unmasking the financial and political hypocrisies of Swedish life. Driven by the desire to reveal the truth as he sees it, he describes with realistic detail, realistic yet impressionistic, the existence of Sellén, the artist, Olle Montanus, the self-taught philosopher and sculptor, Rehnhjelm, the actor, and the practical Lundell, who paints altar-pieces, because they pay well. Strindberg does not, like Zola, analyse his scenes as if he were making a business inventory of the furniture, the costumes, the individuals. Rather, he seizes on the significant detail, the patch of colour, just as he does in his plays, and works them up, obtaining his effect by exaggeration. Read for example the very amusing account of Sellén's and Montanus's shift to keep cold and hunger at bay, when they go to bed in the abandoned photographic studio. As no more planks remain in the floor for firewood, they tuck themselves up in bed with bits of old canvas and blankets, and read aloud recipes from a borrowed cookery book. These artists and intellectuals have a very shrewd idea of the material demands made by life, yet, in spite of all disillusionment, the scenes in which they appear have a freshness of their own. Their struggle to survive is contrasted with the behaviour and attitude of the men who are on top of society, that is, those who have the money with which to make themselves obeyed, and even enforce a lip-service respect from their hangers-on, through the blackmailing power of money. Such is the relationship between Carl Nicolaus Falk and his follower Levin, who, after eighteen years as a supernumerary in the Post Office, has been appointed to the permanent service, and finds himself financially even worse off than before, and such, too, that between Falk and Dr Nyström, who, in return for loans of money, eulogises Falk's virtues in verses written to order for festal occasions. Such a capitalist is also Smith, the publisher, and such is the provincial theatre director, who arbitrarily dictates the fortunes of Falander, Rehnhjelm, and the young actress and *demi-mondaine* Agnes.

Strindberg, then, as might have been expected, takes the part of the under-dog—the *déclassé* and unprivileged—but not of the working class as such. Falk, in his descent of the social ladder, engages himself to write for the Socialist paper *The Worker's Banner* (*Arbetarefanan*), and discovers that its editor is a compound of illiteracy, obsequiousness, and aggressiveness, a servile bully. Strindberg makes fun, too, of the meetings arranged by the workers' societies. Falk and Montanus are thrown out of one of these gatherings, after Olle has enraged the audience he is addressing by his outspoken critical comments on Sweden: 'I don't believe I am saying too much, if I maintain that the Swedish nation is an old-fashioned, conceited, slavish, envious, petty, and coarse nation. And for this reason it is going towards its destruction, and that with rapid strides.'[1] Such sentiments recur in Strindberg's *The New State* (*Det nya Riket*), and explain the storm provoked by that work among the *bourgeoisie*.

Strindberg was particularly aware, at the time of writing *The Red Room*, of the economic instability of Sweden in 1878–9. The general crisis of 1878, produced by over-speculation and over-confidence, hit him hard, and a year after his marriage he became bankrupt. Hence the indignant exposures of the shady financial transactions of the Insurance Company 'Triton', the Theatrical Company 'Phoenix', and all the other companies, often founded without any capital, and protected

[1] *S.S* v, 307.

by the connivance or sloth of the State: these exposures tend at times to unbalance the book. For reasons of caution Strindberg pretended that these transactions took place a decade earlier.

As a result of all his disillusionments, among which his frustrating relationship with Beda, the prostitute (*alias* Agnes, the actress, but Falk does not learn of this till later), plays not the least important part, Falk reaches the stage of having a complete breakdown. He has absorbed the pessimistic philosophy of his friends at Bern's, to the point of nihilism, but his sensitive and high-minded nature cannot take it. 'Falk experienced an inexpressible need for fresh air; he opened the window towards the yard, but it was one of those tall, narrow, dark yards, in which you feel immured as if in a grave, and from which you see only a square of sky when you tilt your head back. And he felt as if he were sitting in the depths of his grave, among the smell of spirits and cooking, and celebrating the funeral of his youth, his good intentions and his honour; he tried smelling the lilac, which stood on the table, but it spread only the scent of decay, and he tried once more through the window to fix his eyes on some object that did not inspire him with loathing.'[1]

At this point Arvid is rescued by Borg, the medical student, whom he had met originally at the funeral of Struve's illegitimate child, and with whose help he has borrowed money. Borg is hard, cynical, and yet flexible, prepared to use the tricks his enemies employ, but maintaining his independence, in his own view, by saying what he likes when he likes. In the novel he represents the new scientific approach to life, stripped of all sentimentality: 'As you know, I look at people with

[1] *S.S.* v, 335.

complete indifference; I take them as geological speci-
mens, as minerals; some crystallise in one system, some
in another; why they do, well, that depends on laws or
circumstances before which we must remain indifferent;
I do not shed tears over chalk, because it is not hard as
crystal; and so I cannot call Falk's situation sad; it was
quite simply the result of his temperament (what you
call heart), plus the circumstances produced by his
temperament.'[1] Borg (while based on a living model,
Emil Kléen) also represents one side of Strindberg, an
exaggeration of the tough, detached creature which
Strindberg strove to be, just as Arvid Falk embodies the
naïve and idealistic aspects of his creator, again in an
exaggerated form. Strindberg himself was certainly
much less naïve than his hero, when he first made the
acquaintance of the circle at Bern's. Clearly he was
himself still in a state of transition, when he wrote the
book, renouncing his own dreams only after a struggle.
Borg in some ways strikes one as a more convincingly
drawn character than Arvid, probably because Strindberg generally showed greater skill in portraying the
unpleasant than the attractive.

Borg is good natured enough—and evidently Strindberg sees him as a man of action—to rescue Falk by
taking him away to the skerries (Strindberg's cure for
his own spiritual ills), where he is provided with a tutor's
post for a while, and meanwhile subjected to a harden-
ing-up process by the indefatigable Borg. He is thereby
restored to health and returns to society, with which he
compromises by entering a government department, de-
voting himself to the hobby of numismatics, and getting
engaged. So that Falk, like Olaus Petri, like Strindberg
himself, has recanted (*The Epilogue to the Red Room*

[1] *S.S.* v, 337.

(*Epilog till Röda Rummet*), 1882, depicts Falk married), and, on the whole, the difficult and strained fortunes of many of the Bohemians have reached, at least temporarily, a solution by the end of the book. Yet there is one significant exception. Olle Montanus, the uncouth sculptor, once an adherent of Fichtean idealism, then a follower of Hartmann and other pessimists, drowns himself. Having seen through the futility of life, he voluntarily—and logically—makes an end of it; a degree of logic to which Strindberg himself never attained. He leaves behind a collection of notes, which presumably express Strindberg's own views at the time, among other things on the uselessness of art and the nature of evil.

From this analysis of *The Red Room* it must be clear how loose is the composition of the novel. The tendency to ramble stands out as one of the book's most obvious faults; in fact one may say that it is a proof of Strindberg's verve and vitality that the work does not weary a reader, this fault notwithstanding. Strindberg's prose style carries it along; it is nervous, flexible, and expressive, often picturesque, but not precious, in its selection of images and in its personifications of inanimate matter. The Dickens influence, in characterisation, subject-matter, and style must be acknowledged. Strindberg borrows Dickens's tricks of grotesque portraiture, but not so much directly as *via* Dickens's American imitators, Mark Twain and others, whom he admired indeed too much. From Dickens came the inspiration to write social satire, yet Strindberg remains more personal, and even, paradoxically enough, lyrical, in his attacks. Zola, at this time, he had not yet read, as he was anxious to point out. Flaubert's *Madame Bovary* he knew and admired, and it certainly influenced him. Yet, though *The Red Room* led to Naturalism in Sweden, it was not a Naturalist work; hence, one may say, its lasting charm. For, in spite of the dating of the subject-matter, Strindberg has succeeded in conjuring up, fresh and yet eternal, the atmosphere of Stockholm as it was in the 'sixties (for it is to the buildings, the sights, of his childhood's Stockholm that he returns, however much the political incidents belong to the 'seventies), the narrow streets of *Staden mellan broarna* (The Old Town) and the idyllic pleasures of Humlegården[1] as it was: 'He went past the round-about, and branched into the avenue leading to the theatre; boys who had played truant from school were sitting there, playing tiddly-winks; further along, a painter's lad lay on his back in the grass and looked up at the sky through the high leafy arches; he whistled as blithely as if neither master nor apprentices were waiting for him, while flies and other winged creatures drowned themselves in his paint pots.'[2]

3

Strindberg's second novel did not appear till 1887, some months after it had been finished. *The People of Hemsö* (*Hemsöborna*) was composed at Lindau in Bavaria, between *The Father* and *Le Plaidoyer d'un Fou*, that is, during one of the worst phases of his first marriage. Distance and the suppressed longing for the Stockholm skerries seem to have endowed his memories of them with a quite remarkable clarity, so vivid is his presentation of Kymmendö, or Hemsö, as he christens this haunt of his in the novel. We know that Strindberg had considered writing down his memories from his summers in the skerries, first in autobiographical form, then as short

[1] A park in the centre of Stockholm, replanned between Strindberg's childhood and maturity.
[2] *S.S.* v, 32.

stories in the style of Auerbach. Acquaintance with Gotthelf's novels, while he was living in Switzerland, decided the shape eventually given to the material, a novel about peasant life, Gotthelf's *Uli der Knecht*, being apparently the most immediate model for *The People of Hemsö*. Yet the development and moral issues of the two stories differ: Uli makes good in an aura of respectable virtue; Carlsson, the hero of Strindberg's novel, as we shall see, meets with a more complicated lot. And the great achievement of Strindberg's work lies really in its essential Swedishness, which does not mean that chauvinistic patriotism has sentimentalized or falsified the telling: rather one may say that Strindberg's intimate knowledge and real understanding of the people and scenery which he is describing have crystallized into a story with both regional and national significance, which for this reason has a more universal appeal.

The plot is simple. Carlsson, the *dräng* or farm hand, from Värmland, arrives at the farm in the Stockholm skerries belonging to the widow Flod. Carlsson, being from Värmland, knows nothing about the sea or fishing: he has been engaged to direct the agricultural work and improve the yield of the property.

Gusten, Mrs Flod's son, junior to Carlsson, and an expert in shooting sea-fowl, but in nothing else, regards the newcomer with suspicion. Despite his lack of interest in farming, he has no desire to lose his authority, even temporarily. So begins at once the struggle for power between the two, a struggle set going rather by Gusten than by Carlsson, for the latter, wily and soft-spoken as he is, is anxious to be on good terms with everyone. His plots and plans, indeed, aim ambitiously at an improvement in his own social and financial position, and, when the pretty maid in the neighbouring professor's family, to whom he is attracted, will not take him seriously anyway, he prepares the ground for a marriage with the widow. She, having tasted the bitterness of celibacy during her two years of widowhood, thinks that the young and lively Carlsson will make an attractive husband; besides, with his introduction of the rotation of crops and so on, he has done much to improve the farm. So the wedding of this incongruous pair is celebrated in true rural style in spite of the son's opposition; only Gusten stays away.

Carlsson, so far, has achieved his ambition, at the price, of course, of some mortification of the flesh. But now, as so often happens when human beings are successful, he begins to lose his judgement, he neglects the farm in order to give himself airs as a hunter and sailor; in a business deal with the director of a felspar company, who buys one of the islands on the property, he is cheated, and finds himself a shareholder in a bankrupt business. Meanwhile Gusten bides his time. Mrs Carlsson has a miscarriage; she can have no more children, and remains very delicate, so that Carlsson realises that his position, as a possible widower, is insecure. He persuades his wife, who steadily declines in health, to make a will in his favour: this is overheard by Gusten, who, at this stage, can do nothing to stop it. Then, however, Carlsson spoils his own chances. Just before Christmas he lets his wife catch him making love to one of the maids; she gets up, in fact, and follows them through the snow-covered woods, and, in doing so, contracts pneumonia. She retires to her bed to die, but first calls in Gusten, destroys her will, and arranges with him what is to be done. On his mother's death, the easy-going Gusten suddenly asserts himself, and it is he who decides that, cut off as they are by ice and snow, they must nevertheless take the body to the church for burial. On the hazardous journey by boat through a blizzard, the coffin falls into the sea: Carlsson and Gusten are marooned on the ice; thanks to his strength and his expert knowledge Gusten saves himself, while Carlsson drowns. Thus ends the subterranean struggle that has been waged between them for so long. The hard-drinking, hard-living pastor Nordström utters Carlsson's epitaph in the admirably detached words: 'Look here, Gusten, I think you've been unjust to Carlsson, and I don't know what you mean by his deeds.... Carlsson was a fly chap, and he did everything you would have liked to do, and couldn't.... There are more ways of looking at people than yours.'[1]

In a statement made several years later (in 1894) Strindberg claimed that he had anticipated Nietzsche's conception of the struggle for power in such works (among others) as *The Father* and *The People of Hemsö*, that is, before he had read Nietzsche. Yet one feels that Strindberg, in a sense, is wronging his novel by analysing it in such terms. There is no schematic ideology in the book, and its strength springs from this fact. So often Strindberg was tempted to project his own ideas by creating characters to illustrate them. Here he appears content to draw the people as he knew them, and to let them speak and act really 'in character'. Only occasionally does an exaggerated gesture or word jar, in the otherwise well-balanced whole. From the technical point of view the fact that Carlsson is a landlubber, a foreigner in the little community, provides Strindberg with an excellent means of contrasting the quick, talkative, Värmland opportunist with the dourer and more taciturn people of the islands, and provides, too, convincing

[1] *S.S.* xxi, 174.

motivation through character for the development of
the action. Note that it is the slow-witted, patient Gusten
who wins in the end. Strindberg exercises unusual
objectivity in his handling of Carlsson in defeat. There
is a kind of lazy, 'Irish' easy-goingness about him,
which rounds him off artistically. He manifests his non-
chalance, for instance, at the wedding, when, after a
Gargantuan drinking-bout, the pastor is found asleep in
the marriage-bed. By dint of considerable ingenuity the
pastor is manœuvred out of the bed and into the muddy
sea, after which Carlsson pretends to rescue him: 'casting up his eyes to heaven, and lamenting in broken
dialect, as he always did when he wished to make a
plausible and gentle impression: "Would you believe it,
that as I was walking down here, quite by chance, I heard
something splashing and wailing, so that I thought it was
a seal; and then I saw it was our own little pastor." [1]

The wedding scene ranks as one of Strindberg's
masterpieces of satiric, realistic description of incident
and character; the tightly laced, elderly bride in white,
already pregnant, anxiously hangs back in the hope that
her resentful son will arrive before the service starts; the
service itself, which is interrupted by the popping of innumerable corks, for the beer-bottles, lying in the sun
outside, in readiness for the wedding breakfast, are ex-
ploding in the heat; then the coffee-drinking and punch-
quaffing before the main meal starts in the twilight, while
Japanese lanterns are hung up in the trees and the girls
set out enormous dishes of delicacies. By the time the
pastor rises to address the guests, he has already, led on
by Carlsson, drunk so much that he has become confused as to the nature of the occasion, and begins a
Christmas homily: 'My friends, when the first snow....' [2]

[1] *S.S.* XXI, 135.   [2] *S.S.* XXI, 130.

Yet even into this coarse and grotesque scene Strindberg has brought in as relief the beauty of the Swedish summer, the coolness of the dewy grass, and the scent of hay. For, whether in its garb of ice and snow, or in its adornment of young birch leaves and lilac, nature remains the ever-changing but ever-present factor in this narrative of the Hemsö people, on land and on sea.

In spite of the tragic ending, Strindberg considered that *The People of Hemsö* was a cheerful, almost too cheerful, book. In its lack of polemical intention it differed both from much of his other work and from the remaining Swedish literature of the 'eighties, the phase of literature that had been inaugurated by *The Red Room*. By the time he composed this novel of rustic life, his earlier enthusiasm for Rousseau and country life had been considerably modified, a fact which partially explains Strindberg's objectivity in his character-drawing.

4

Before Strindberg had finished *In the Outer Skerries* (*I Havsbandet*), in 1890, his views had changed even further. Begun in the summer of 1889, this work was not completed till June 1890—an unusually protracted period of incubation for Strindberg. He had started on the book whilst alone at Runmarö, separated from wife and children, but in the course of the year the imminence of the divorce, which he now feared, seems to have unbalanced him further, and his second sojourn at Runmarö, during the summer of 1890, filled him with increasing gloom. *In the Outer Skerries* bears strong resemblances, so far as setting and personalities are concerned, to *The People of Hemsö*, but the author's attitude to his material has undergone a very marked change: he now evinces a sharp hostility to the population of the islands. As in the earlier novel the arrival of the 'foreigner' Carlsson, *der Bote von der Aussenwelt*, precipitates the action, so here it is the coming of Borg, the *fiskeri intendent* (inspector of fisheries) and his clash with his surroundings, which form the plot. Borg (who has no connection with his namesake of *The Red Room*) is depicted as an intellectual, a scientist, who, like his creator, has failed to achieve recognition by the Academies, but none the less is superior to them, and *a fortiori* to the stupid and humble people who surround him. In effect, he personifies the conception Strindberg held at this time of the 'Superman', an idea formed first independently and then under the influence of Nietzsche.

Typical of his creator's admiration, at this time, for science, as opposed to the arts, is the fact that, like the Captain in *The Father*, Borg is represented as a scientist. He has been sent to investigate the reasons for the decline in the herring fishing round the skerries. Naturally, as an 'official', he is regarded with suspicion and dislike by the inhabitants. 'Are they rising well?' he asks a fisherman, on his first stroll round the island. 'Not yet, but I suppose they will now that the Government's in on it',[1] answers the fisherman ironically. Borg displays all his scientific skill in testing the water, soil deposits, and so on, meanwhile alienating the local people increasingly by his arrogance, for he behaves as an aristocrat towards his inferiors. Thus, despite his quick wit and ingenious theories, his Poe-Dupin power of reading other people's thoughts, and his displays of almost magic skill, he fails partially in his mission, which was designed as well to induce the fisher-people to adopt

[1] *S.S.* xxiv, 27.

more modern methods in their work. Meanwhile, he
has taken up with a young lady, Maria, to whom he gets
engaged, while realising that he is thereby being false to
his own principle of contempt for women of her kind;
he then discovers that she is faithless, and, after seducing
her, an operation in which she appears to participate
readily enough, breaks off the engagement and lives in
solitude. He now devotes himself to scientific experiments, even trying to make a homunculus in a glass
bottle (cf. Goethe's *Faust*, Part II). Finally, dismissed
as he has been from his post, driven to madness by his
isolation on the island and the persecution he suffers at
the inhabitants' hands, he goes off sailing alone, one
Christmas Eve, in search of death.

Strindberg paints a terrifying picture of Borg in his
misery and degradation, when the children stone him,
and he totters round, dirty, exhausted from hunger, a
wreck of a man. Such details of degeneration occur frequently in the Zola novels; and clearly Zola's influence
has here left its mark, not only in this respect, but in
Strindberg's approach to nature. Not always, but all
too often, his fresh appreciation of form and colour and
sound gives way to a would-be scientific analysis of the
component parts of the scene he describes, as for instance
in the following passage: 'When he had climbed up
between the sharp stones, and reached the top, it was as
if he had accomplished an Alpine ascent in ten minutes.
The belt of deciduous trees lay beneath him, and on the
mountain plateau the Alpine flora showed itself...
beside the genuinely Northern cloud-berry in the damp
crevices of the peat-moss, and in amongst them the little
cornus, perhaps the only Swedish and the only skerry
plant'[1]...and so on. Even though marred by this

[1] *S.S.* xxiv, 79.

pseudo-scientific approach—and later critics have indicated the inaccurate nature of some of Strindberg's marine biology, a criticism which cannot be levelled at his technical accounts of sailing—Strindberg's flexible prose remains a saving grace.

Borg in a state of physical and mental decay contrasts poignantly with the elegant and cool-headed savant who first makes his appearance in the opening scene: 'The little gentleman wore a light beaver-coloured coat, below which a pair of wide moss-green trousers of jersey material showed, opening over a pair of crocodile leather boots, with black buttons....His face, what could be seen of it, was thin and dead white, and a small thin black moustache with curly ends accentuated his pallor, and gave an exotic touch to his expression.'[1] In the description of his books and possessions in a later chapter, this elegance and fastidiousness again receive emphasis. Strindberg's hero, indeed, is depicted as a dandy, an aesthete, scientist though he is, and displays certain similarities with the Parisian dandy of Baudelaire and Huysmans. Curiously enough (and this provides a further link with French aestheticism), he champions the cause of Roman Catholicism, though he himself is an atheist, on the grounds of the cultural value of the Catholic faith.

These conflicting strains make Borg interesting, but not convincing, and withal slightly comic—that most fatal characteristic for the hero of a novel. Strindberg's intellectual Superman—deliberately represented as a physical weakling—is ruined by the stupidity of his fellow-creatures; only at the end, in his madness, does he attain to the stature of a tragic hero, recalling the fate of Nietzsche, which may well have inspired

[1] *S.S.* xxiv, 5, 6.

Strindberg's conclusion. Obviously Strindberg's own discords, his monomaniac hatred of woman, inspired by his dependence on her, are all reflected in the development of the book. Unfortunately *In the Outer Skerries*, whilst offering much fascinating material on Strindberg's state of mind in 1890, and some interesting evidence concerning his transition from his particular brand of Naturalism, does not succeed in its objective of making the character of a genius take life before our eyes.

5

The two remaining novels, *The Gothic Rooms* (*Götiska Rummen*) and *Black Banners* (*Svarta Fanor*), were both written in 1904, though the latter was not published till three years later, a delay due to difficulty in finding a publisher, and to the advice of Strindberg's friends. The title of *The Gothic Rooms* refers back to *The Red Room*; the former meeting-place of the circle had been altered and redecorated, and twenty-five years later the members meet again, together with additions such as Dr Borg's nephew, the architect. A party in these rooms serves as introduction, just as another party forms the conclusion. Otherwise Strindberg bothers little about the claims of composition, and launches into a general attack on the decadence of Swedish society at the *fin de siècle*, a parallel to his onslaught in *The Red Room*, but lacking the earlier book's force and piquancy. Much of what he has to say is given in the form of rather tedious diatribes, or arguments. In *The Red Room* Strindberg had made his social and intellectual criticism vivid by his illustrations of the abuses prevailing; here he tends to be boring. He had changed many of his views since 1879; he was now a Christian mystic and no longer a positivist; but he still distrusted and hated emancipated women, indeed, was now openly at war with them, and *The Gothic Rooms* is full of incidents of broken marriages, ascribed to the dangerous influence of feminist doctrines. Dr Borg no longer receives visits from female patients; his reputation is blasted, since he has told too many women that their nervous condition has been caused by an unnatural life, no children, abortions, birth control. Strindberg's tone is often extremely coarse, nevertheless, in his usual paradoxical manner, he represents the one idealized relationship in the book, that between Count Max and Ester, the woman doctor, who is finally to be saved from a career by marriage, as one of spiritual rather than physical love—that is, Strindberg blames the carnal aspects of love for the discords arising in the relationship between man and woman.

The pessimism and misanthropy exuded by Strindberg in *The Gothic Rooms* found a far more virulent expression in *Black Banners*, which is truly a masterpiece of invective. It is a pity that much of the satire, being aimed at a definite set and time, should thus be necessarily restricted in scope, and the book dated accordingly. After the first limited edition had proved a *succès de scandale*, and been sold out, Strindberg was asked whether he would not consent to a second edition 'för välgörande ändamål' (for charity). He replied: '*Svarta Fanor är* utgiven för välgörande ändamål' ('*Black Banners has* been published for—a good cause'). The anecdote, with its unrenderable play on words, casts a significant light on Strindberg's desire to castigate. In *Black Banners* he arbitrarily put together two works planned separately; the novel concerning Zachris, Jenny, and Falkenström, and their circle, and the dialogues on occult phenomena intended as a continuation of the conversations between Max and Ester in *The Gothic Rooms*. The conception of an undenominational monastery (as in *To Damascus III*), to which Max and later Falkenström retire, furnishes the pretext for these high-faluting conversations, in which Strindberg is very much in earnest. Nothing, however, could strike a more discordant note in these spiritual harmonies than the satirical exposure, in the author's most grotesque manner, of the life led in a certain section of contemporary Stockholm society. His chief victim, Zachris, was a portrait of the novelist Gustaf af Geijerstam, as Strindberg saw him. Geijerstam[1] had used his own marriage with a consumptive as material, in romanticized form, for novels; Strindberg takes a devilish delight in exposing this romantic fiction as a distortion of the truth; in Zachris[2] and his wife Jenny, dissipated, futile, dishonest, and perpetually battening on other people, their ideas, their money, their friends, Strindberg has drawn two successful caricatures of unsurpassed malice. Strindberg's description of Jenny's death-bed (Geijerstam's wife had died at the turn of the century) is in extremely bad taste, even if Geijerstam, by his rather maudlin sentimental revelations of his own family life, had laid himself open to attack. Hanna Paj, with her red nose and insidious intrigues, represents Ellen Key, that active apostle of female emancipation, who was one of Strindberg's bugbears. Like horrid phantoms the whole set is assembled and exposed in the first chapter at the dinner party in Professor Stenkåhl's house, a *spökdiné*, prototype of the scene in *The Ghost Sonata*.

---

[1] Apparently Strindberg partly modelled the figure of the Captain in *The Dance of Death* on Geijerstam.

[2] The figure of Zachris, the literary parasite, was evidently suggested to Strindberg by E. T. A. Hoffmann's 'Klein Zaches'. Cf. *Black Banners* (*S.S.* xli, 271) and Lamm, *August Strindberg*, ii, 259 ff.

Over and above the immediate literary caricatures, Strindberg attacked the futility of an author's life as such, the incessant need to produce 'copy' out of his own life and emotions, a criticism levelled at himself too in the person of Falkenström, and this links the book up with his ideas in *The Red Room* and other works of the 'eighties. Strindberg also seized on the general trend of Swedish life as he saw it, its increasing materialism; it was, after all, this materialism which had helped to bring about the decadence of the literary circles. He exposes, too, the hold of materialism on society in general. Through this, Strindberg's novel, in spite of the ephemeral nature of the literary squabbles it denounces, has maintained a certain permanent value as a *description de mœurs*.

As a novelist, Strindberg never achieved all that *The Red Room* had promised. One might say that his tendency to loose composition, sketchy characterization, exaggerated grotesqueness, gained the upper hand: moreover, tormented by persecution and lack of appreciation, he used the novel more and more as an instrument for literary 'execution', to employ his own term. Only *The People of Hemsö* can be excepted from these strictures. It is worth noting that *The People of Hemsö* is usually considered to be one of Strindberg's least characteristic works in any *genre*.

CHAPTER VII

THE SHORT STORIES

WHAT has been said in the preceding Chapter concerning the slow development of the Swedish novel may be taken also to cover the short story, the *novell*, a term in Swedish including both the short story proper and the 'long short story', as the German Romantic writers in particular had cultivated them. On the whole, the Swedish Romantic writers, like the Germans, accomplished more in the genre of the *novell* than they did in the novel. Frederika Bremer's *début* as a writer (see above, Chapter VI, p. 148) was made with a series of short stories called *Sketches from Everyday Life (Teckningar från Vardagslivet)*, mediocre in themselves, and interesting only in the choice of realistic family life as subject-matter. I have already indicated the services rendered by C. J. L. Almquist in the development of the *novell* and in making it a vehicle for ideas and an instrument for polemics. In both these aspects the *genre* was to be taken up by Strindberg and endowed with greater force and range.

The volume *Town and Gown* has been discussed above. With that work and other earlier sketches published in *At the Coming of Spring (I Vårbrytningen)* Strindberg had completed his apprenticeship. His next collection, *Swedish Destinies and Adventures (Svenska Öden och Äventyr)*, of which Part I appeared in 1882 and Part II in the following year, contains some of the best stories (in their way) that he ever wrote. Strindberg had become increasingly absorbed in Swedish history through his studies for *The Swedish People on Holy Days and Working*

Days (*Svenska Folket i Hälg och Söcken*), and, as has already been noted, had by this time already written several historical dramas. As in his plays, so he uses these stories of the Middle Ages and the sixteenth century to embody modern ideas, and to debate contemporary problems. Social questions, at this period of Strindberg's life, were assuming more and more importance in his eyes. Thus, the first story of all, *Cultivated Fruit (Odlad Frukt)*, takes up the problem of the over-educated aristocratic youth with no money, who is totally unfit to cope with the practical task of earning his living, and is driven in the end to commit suicide, since society can offer him no place in its ordered hierarchy. Here Strindberg takes up the Darwinian doctrine of the survival of the fittest, but is influenced as well by his own experiences of the Swedish educational system of the 'sixties and 'seventies. Yet, apart from these sociological aspects, the portrait of young Sir Sten, the hero, the last, and ruined, descendant of the Ulvfot family, who in 1460 rides away from his bankrupt property, interests and convinces as that of an aristocratic *Junker* at grips with life in Stockholm. All Strindberg's imagination—and it was a powerful one—is revealed in such scenes as the description of the wedding dance, or of the public bath-house, where Sten is surrounded by the burghers and artisans of the capital. Such use of realistic detail recurs throughout these stories, and impresses as one of Strindberg's chief assets in recreating history. It is seen again, for instance, in *Development (Utveckling)*, with its descriptions of the coming of the plague to Gripsholm, an incident in the story of the Renaissance painter Botvid, who is torn between idealism and the desire to enjoy life in all its fulness. Botvid's complicated character is contrasted with the spontaneous sensuality of Giacomo, who paints the Madonna in the form of his black-haired mistress, Maria. Strindberg, though only an amateur, was himself a painter, a fact of which one is constantly reminded in his descriptions, from *The Red Room* onwards. The poignant and well-written *Higher Purposes* (*Högre Ändamål*) describes the decree of the Roman Church issued during the Middle Ages forbidding priests to marry or continue in wedlock, as it affects one happy clerical family; the man becomes sick and half-crazy, and is restored only by the return of his wife, now no longer his legal spouse, and his two children. He defies excommunication by the Church, and goes away to start a new life. Typical of the hypocrisy of the Church (any official Church, and specifically the Swedish Lutheran Church), in Strindberg's view, was the later unofficial modification of the ban: a cleric could take as mistress, under the guise of housekeeper, any woman except his former wife.

These stories were very well received; they were read as historical narratives, not as attacks on contemporary society, and their popularity as such seems actually to have irritated Strindberg.

A third volume of similar stories appeared in 1890–1, and included *A Witch* (*En Häxa*), really a rewriting in historical form of a modern short story, *Short Cuts* (*Genvägar*) of 1887, in which Strindberg analysed the character of a lower-class woman, lazy, lustful, and hysterical, who attempts to dominate her environment by laying claim to supernatural powers. In the historical version the story gains in power; Thekla, the heroine, gives false evidence of witchcraft against the young Countess who has befriended her, and is herself arrested and brought before the justices. Imagining that she is going to be put to the torture, she dies, of shock—

another instance of Strindberg's interest in the problem of suggestion, which has already been noted in the plays of this period, for example *Lady Julia, Pariah*, and *Simoon*. Another story, which was first printed separately in Danish, and later added to the revised edition of *Swedish Destinies* in the collected works, was *Tschandala*. Here again the conception of the plot and of the characterisation was modern, based, in fact, on an experience of Strindberg himself during his stay at Skovlyst outside Copenhagen in 1888 (see above, Chapter II, p. 44): the feud between himself and the gipsy steward of the estate. Strindberg had accused the steward of theft: the steward accused Strindberg of seducing his sister. Strindberg sets the whole story in the seventeenth century, depicts his own role (taken over in the story by the worthy Doctor Törner) in a much more favourable light, and lets the conflict take place between the Doctor and the gipsy steward of the crazy Baroness in a decaying manor house outside Lund in South Sweden. The atmosphere of this place, with its over-grown garden and ruined buildings, is particularly well described, but Strindberg's *forte*, it should be remembered, lay in evoking the disagreeable in all its complexity. In the end the Doctor, with his superior intelligence, outwits the criminal gipsy, reduces him to a state of terror by suggestion, and then lets the starved dogs of the house tear him to pieces—one of the most brutal assertions of the right of the stronger to be found in all Strindberg's works.

This story reveals in an exaggerated, and therefore infelicitous, form the conception inspiring these volumes, that the past is in no way a piece of venerable antiquity, the personalities and ideals of which must be represented in the old, time-honoured way, but simply a more distant part of the present, inhabited by people subject to the same laws as men of to-day. This conception links these stories with the historical plays, and explains, for instance, the stripping of Charles XII, after his death, in *At the Wake in Tistedal* (*Vid Likvakan i Tistedalen*), of all pretensions to rank as a national hero.

Long before he wrote these later historical stories, Strindberg had launched out into the modern short story proper with *Married* (*Giftas*), volume I, in 1884.

The stories in *Married*, volume I, all embody different aspects of the problems raised by marriage—economic, social, or emotional—and form Strindberg's most effective contribution to the discussion of feminist questions. It seems ironic that the book should ever have been threatened with confiscation, even on the technical ground that a passage in the first story, *The Reward of Virtue* (*Dygdens Lön*), was blasphemous; for Strindberg's attitude to love and marriage, as exemplified in these stories, is fundamentally moral: moral, that is, in taking the problems connected with marriage seriously, and in showing up the hypocrisy of many of society's conventions. Strindberg does not (as yet) desire to destroy the institution of marriage; on the contrary, it is just because he believes in its possibilities and in the importance of motherhood, that he has so little patience with what he considers to be distortions of nature.

These views are aired, with considerable polemical skill, in the two prefaces, in the second of which Strindberg analyses Ibsen's *Doll's House*, and comes to the conclusion that it is a specious plea for a special case. The most amusing and successful of the stories in *Married* bears the same title as Ibsen's play, namely *Ett Dockhem*, and is clearly designed to make fun of the pretensions of emancipated women, who devote their lives to higher learning, and lose all contact with real life. The story concerns a naval captain and his wife Gurli, who have been happily married for many years, and are surrounded by a flock of healthy children. Every year the Captain has to go off on a cruise; and, every time he returns, his wife meets him at Dalarö, in the Stockholm *skärgård*, and they celebrate their reunion as if they were newly married. In the description of these meetings at the old inn by the sea, where the two dine and then spend the night in an enormous old-fashioned double bed, till the Captain has to return, in the very early summer dawn, to his ship, as the waking gulls cry and a red light illumines the rocks, Strindberg achieved some of his best prose. He captures, too, the harmony, the camaraderie, and the physical satisfaction desirable for a happy marriage. At this period of his life, he knew what he wanted for himself, even if in his own relationships he never achieved it.

The Paradise in the story is then disturbed by a serpent, in the shape of an old maid, Ottilia, who, during one of these periodic absences of the bluff, honest Captain, gets to know Gurli, and fills her head with ideas about the emancipation of women, and about religion. Gurli now has doubts of the 'rightness' of her marriage. It has been too 'earthly', as she describes it in a letter to her astonished husband. She reads Ibsen's *Doll's House*, and takes her husband's criticisms of that work hardly: on his return home this time, all the family assemble to meet him at Dalarö, including the bobbed Ottilia—no dallying in the moonlight this time—and so things go from bad to worse, till the Captain seeks the advice of his wise mother-in-law, and pays court to the withered old spinster, discusses astronomy with her up to all hours of the night, sees her home, holds her hand, and in fact succeeds in his game, which is to make his wife thoroughly jealous. Gurli quarrels with Ottilia, emancipation is dropped, and harmony is restored in the Captain's house. This story, deliberately naïve as it is in many ways, is written with a happy combination of humour and satire, with the freshness of the sea as background.

Of the other stories, many of which, it must be confessed, have dated considerably, *No Choice* (*Måste*), the description of a hardened bachelor's descent into wedlock, is one of the most successful, in its evocation of Stockholm atmosphere. Very different, in their harshness and total lack of detachment, are the stories in *Married*, volume II, written in June 1885, and provoked by the storm over the preceding volume. The violent preface sets the tone for the narratives, in which the female sex is depicted as entirely venal, hypocritical, and selfish. For instance, the heroine in *For Payment* (*Mot Betalning*), who has certain similarities to Ibsen's Hedda Gabler,[1] sells her favours to her husband, a politician, the price being her liberty to interfere in his political decisions.

The other volume of this period, *Real Utopias* (*Utopier i Verkligheten*), was not published till after *Married*, volume I, though most of its contents were actually written in 1884, when Strindberg still retained a very strong positive belief in the value of Socialism, in respect of which he followed along the lines of Rousseau, not Marx, and took up French and Russian Utopian theories. Even at this stage of his development Strindberg found it difficult to suppress his non-Naturalist, or

---

[1] Sten Linder, in the book of essays, *Ibsen, Strindberg och Andra*, p. 88, argues that Ibsen was influenced by Strindberg in his conception of Hedda.

Romantic, tendencies, and his longing to believe in a personal God, as the four stories in *Utopias* bear witness. Here Strindberg deals with social problems in a contemporary setting (Switzerland, and in one instance France), but the thesis of the historical story *Cultivated Fruit* (see above, p. 175) is repeated in the Preface's opening lines: 'This book is an attack on "over-culture", or degeneration.'[1] Strindberg was careful to stress that not culture but 'excess of culture' formed the object of his attack. 'We have become too delicate, therefore coarseness is a symptom of social regression. It is delicate to lie, and coarse to say what one thinks. Let us educate ourselves to more coarseness.'[2] But even the Preface, written after the stories, and in some respects more positive than they are, does not expound the belief that evolution necessarily tends towards a better state, nor that the strong always survive, nor does Strindberg believe that nature is always happy and peaceful.

In the stories themselves the complexity of the impulses revealed, rather than any convincing force in the arguments, provides the interest. Thus Paul Petrowitsch, the hero of *Relapse* (*Återfall*), a Russian revolutionary author who has taken refuge on the shores of the Lake of Geneva outside Lausanne, is torn between irrational longing for his own country, where he was a gentleman, and respect for his adopted one, where he is a gardener, between the desire to tear down all the old castes and conventions that have enslaved society, and sympathy and love for his companion and mistress, Anna, who, despite their agreement not to marry and all their revolutionary tenets, wishes to have her newborn son christened. Indeed, at one point, during a temporary absence from Anna, Paul even starts to

[1] *S.S.* xv, 5.   [2] *S.S.* xv, 9.

sympathise with an elderly Catholic priest, whom he sees ill-treated by his young pupil. Eventually, however, Anna and Paul continue in their striving to prepare a new society for the coming generation. The end is the least effective part of the story, as is that of *Rebuilding* (*Nybyggnad*), the weakest and most doctrinaire in the book, in which the heroine, Blanche, a doctor and as such an emancipated woman, eventually finds love and happiness in the phalanstery at Guise, run on the principles of Fourier, where the economic and practical difficulties of marriage are disposed of, so as to permit harmonious relationships.

In *Pangs of Conscience* (*Samvetskval*), the hero, Von Bleichroder, a German, and by profession a geologist, is serving as a lieutenant in the 1870 war against France. When the story opens, he is stationed near Fontaine-bleau, and is there given orders to shoot certain captured *francs-tireurs*. Divided between his feelings as a sensitive man and his duties as a German citizen and Prussian officer, Von Bleichroder makes arrangements for the execution of the three Frenchmen, but, after it has taken place, and he has himself returned from an aimless reconnaissance in the Forest of Fontainebleau, collapses, and develops acute schizophrenia. The analysis of this mental crisis, led up to in the macabre conversation between the French peasant landlady and the lieutenant, who discusses his own body in his bed, as if it were a third person—'But he seems very ill, and probably ought to have a doctor'[1]—and culminating in the talk with the French pastor, after which Von Bleichroder throws himself out of the window, is very skilfully and movingly done. Strindberg succeeds, too, in conveying the sharpness of the young man's mental re-

[1] *S.S.* xv, 195.

actions by the intensity of his physical responses. As he roams round the Fontainebleau forests, Von Bleichroder becomes uneasily aware of the dogged, cunning struggle going on in nature between different forces, tree fighting against tree for life. On his return to his quarters he notices something that looks like red clusters of grapes round the vine stock in the courtyard, red silhouetted against the white wall, the red of the human blood which has just been shed. This red recurs in the radishes laid out for his supper, and in the wine standing on the table. No one scene in Strindberg's stories surpasses, in psychological truth, the climax in *Pangs of Conscience*. It is a pity that the second part of the story should fall off, becoming too facile; for the lieutenant recovers in a Swiss asylum, under the care of a doctor who is a disciple of Jean-Jacques Rousseau, and he and his wife, in due course, become Swiss citizens and supporters of the ideal of international peace.

It has been noted that in *The People of Hemsö* Strindberg had already abandoned his Rousseauistic views on peasant life, and saw his subjects realistically. In the collection *The Life of the Men of the Skerries (Skärkarlsliv)*, which, in story form, deals with the same background as *The People of Hemsö*, a more sombre note is struck. *A Criminal (En Brottsling)*, for instance, describes the trial of a man who, by his own confession, has murdered his wife, after seventeen years of marriage. The man refuses to give any reason for his action; only comments by the local doctor and a juror indicate that the subnormal wife was the real criminal.

The grim taciturnity of this hero forms a marked contrast to the gentle dreaminess of Alrik Lundstedt, the central figure of *The Romantic Sacristan of Rånö (Den romantiske Klockaren på Rånö)*, the 'long short story' in this

volume. In face of the poverty and hunger of his childhood, and the memory of his father's killing of his
mother, which he witnessed, Alrik has taken refuge in
a life of imagination, in which he 'pretends', and the
most insignificant object provokes fantastic and happy
dreams. Strindberg certainly introduces autobiographical material into this story. Alrik succeeds in making his
way to the Musical Academy in Stockholm, and hopes
to train as a musician, but his father's extravagance and
profligacy oblige him to cut short his training, and, after
qualifying as an organist, to retire as sacristan to the
little island of Rånö, where his duties as organist and
schoolmaster combined leave him ample leisure to
dream about the beautiful Angelika whom he will one
day marry. In this gift of vivid fantasy he resembles
more particularly, as has been pointed out, the student
hero of E. T. A. Hoffmann's *Goldener Topf*. His power of
escape in this way is, however, at one stage cut short, for
a certain experience reminds him of the past, and he is
overcome by a feeling of guilt about his mother's death;
yet, after the pastor has urged on him the consolations
of Christianity, which he accepts in his own simplified
version, he rediscovers his gift of fantasy, gets married
happily, and blithely embroiders on his stories both for
himself and others.

There is thus very little incident in this tale, yet with
its graceful and curious mingling of the fantastic and
the realistic (which recalls Almquist's *noveller*) *The
Sacristan of Rånö* occupies a place of its own in Strindberg's writings, not least interesting in that this 'romantic' *novell* was written in the middle of Strindberg's
so-called Naturalist period, and was followed by such
works as *Lady Julia* and *Creditors*. Strindberg was later
persistently to point out that he had written it well be-

fore the manifesto[1] of Heidenstam and Levertin against the prevailing *skomakarrealism* (cobbler's realism).

Fagervik and Skamsund (*Fagervik och Skamsund*) was planned as a further volume of skerry stories, but during the composition of it Strindberg used up a number of its original themes in *The Dream Play*,[2] and, in any case, by this date (1902) his approach to the material had changed again. The finished volume, therefore, has a heterogeneous character. It contains, apart from a few slight sketches, and some attractive poetry, as *pièces de résistance* (in the author's view at least) *The Quarantine-Master's Stories* (*Karantänmästarns Berättelser*), two long *noveller* built up on autobiographical material. The second of these, which Strindberg had actually planned and begun as a novel (*The Monastery* (*Klostret*), 1898), was the narrative of his second marriage. Places and names have been changed from Germany and Austria to Denmark, but so unconvincingly that his contemporaries must have recognised the persons concerned without any difficulty. The stories in *Fagervik and Skamsund* have more autobiographical than aesthetic interest.

The little volume *Sagor* (*Fairy-Tales*), published the following year (1903), reflects the sunnier moods inspired in Strindberg by Harriet Bosse, but also the bitterness of parting from her; these personal sources, however, are veiled by the fairy-tale form which Strindberg employs. Markedly influenced as they are by Hans Andersen, they yet have a charm of their own, derived in part at least from Strindberg's genuine love for flowers and things of nature, and his interest (revealed in so many of his writings after the Inferno Crisis) in trying to

[1] This manifesto, *Pepitas Bröllop*, was published in 1890.
[2] See, for instance, the scenes between the Quarantine-Master, the Officer and Indra's Daughter, etc., in that play, *S.S.* xxxvi, 264–78.

explain the workings of nature in mystical-scientific terms. In the realm of fairy stories these fantastic phenomena seem quite acceptable, and they have the attractive, naïve colouring of a Carl Larsson picture. This charm appears perhaps most happily in *Bluewing finds the Golden Saxifrage* (*Blåvingen finner Guldpudran*), where the constancy of the little girl Bluewing, in her search for the precious herb that marks a well, forms the theme. Read, for instance, the following passage: 'The roof [of the old man's house] consisted of creepers; virginia creeper, honeysuckle, clematis, ivy; growing so thickly that not a drop of rain could penetrate. Outside the door hives were ranged, but instead of bees there were butterflies. It was a beautiful sight when they swarmed. "I don't like to torment bees", said the old man. "Besides, they are so ugly, they look like hairy coffee-beans, and they sting, too, like vipers."'[1]

In *The Trials of the Pilot* (*Lotsens Vedermödor*) Strindberg introduces the humorously fantastic, as cover for the moral. Some of the other tales, unfortunately, remain prosaically close to the every-day world, or else the satire in them verges on the obvious, as in *Philosophy and Photography* (*Filosofi och Fotografi*).

The two *berättelser* (tales), as Strindberg described them, *The Roofing Spree* (*Taklagsöl*)[2] and *The Scapegoat* (*Syndabocken*), approximating to *noveller* in length, have sometimes been referred to as novels proper, but appear to lack the weight necessary for such classification. Strindberg originally planned the two as one work. In *The Roofing Spree* the hero, the curator, lying

---

[1] *S.S.* xxxviii, 114.
[2] The title refers to the completion of a building opposite the curator's home, which will block his view of the house where his chief enemy lives. As the curator dies, he hears the distant shouts of the workmen during the roofing ceremony.

on his deathbed, doped with morphia after an accident, looks back on his past life, experiencing again the sorrows of losing his wife and child (this theme which recurs so often, so obsessionally, in Strindberg's works), and tasting again past insults and hates, but also past joys. Alternating at first between bouts of delirium and calmer moments when he continues to cling to life, he finally dies peacefully. This story, written as an almost uninterrupted monologue, derives its chief interest from its technique: the variations of tone and mood, in the stream of reminiscences which literally pour from the dying man's lips and which exercise an almost horrible fascination, like the Ancient Mariner's eye.

The Scapegoat, possibly influenced by Balzac's choice of subject-matter, bourgeois existence, describes life in a small town; Lund and Uppsala had probably served as models. The two main characters are Askanius, the extravagant owner of a large hotel, and his friend Libotz, the lawyer; in fact the kind of characters to whom Balzac was attracted. Askanius' megalomaniac plans have brought him to ruin, but he refuses to yield to fate, and on Christmas Eve he sits alone in his gigantic restaurant drinking champagne. This macabre scene is undeniably effective. The honest lawyer, who is always being blamed and insulted, and flexibly yields to the various forms of pressure applied to him, is a very different and, as portrayed here, a less convincing character. In the end he is forced to leave the town and seek his fortune elsewhere. It is clear that, at any rate sometimes, Strindberg saw himself as a similar, innocent, scapegoat.

Strindberg probably found it easier to write short stories than novels, since from one point of view at least, though for quite different reasons, the same criticism may be levelled against him as against Alfred de Vigny: 'il a le souffle court'. Vigny wrote little as a result of this weakness; Strindberg, instead, tended to repeat himself. This tendency mars even some of his best stories, which contain extremely vivid scenes, and, almost without exception, are written in living and elegant prose.

CHAPTER VIII

THE AUTOBIOGRAPHICAL
WRITINGS

IT must be fairly obvious from what has already been said that most of Strindberg's original works are very largely based on his own experiences. And, if Goethe's works were, as he claimed, 'Bruchstücke einer grossen Konfession', Strindberg's may equally be designated fragments of a confession, but very often of a slight or trivial confession. Nevertheless, among the groups of Strindberg's writings which must be considered there is also one which consists of autobiographical works of the most direct kind, though diverse in form and type.

Of this group the first example (apart from certain uncompleted fragments and articles), and in many ways the most striking, is *The Son of the Bondwoman* (*Tjänstekvinnans Son*), the four parts of which, begun in 1886, were completed, with the rapidity so characteristic of its author, within the same year. Clearly a pretty powerful impulse to dwell on his own past sufferings and joys, but more especially his sufferings and the psychological development linked with them, must have inspired this re-living of his life from his birth in 1849 up to the time of writing in 1886,[1] and, though Strindberg does not actually claim to give an account of his own birth-pangs and the discomforts of teething, he does, in the famous first chapter of the first volume, *Hungry and Afraid* (*Rädd och Hungrig*), give a vivid description of the *malaises* of life

---

[1] 1887 is the year actually cited as the terminal point, as Strindberg got the fourth volume of the work ready for publication that year. In fact *The Author* was not printed till 1909.

affecting the tiny Johan. The substitution of Johan, Strindberg's first baptismal name, for August provides the most obvious concession to the fictional form; the hero Johan, too, is always referred to in the third person. Strindberg alters the names of places and persons, but otherwise these four volumes, which as they stand might rank as a novel, are simply the story of Strindberg's childhood, youth, and manhood, as they unfold themselves against the background of contemporary Sweden. The only factor of importance omitted is the development of the relationship with Siri—a considerable omission, to be sure; only the first meeting with her, that lovely spring afternoon in the Stockholm street, is reported, in the third volume, *In the Red Room* (*I Röda Rummet*), and their subsequent marriage is mentioned in the fourth volume, *The Author* (*Författaren*). But Strindberg has often mixed up dates in his narrative; for the first two volumes he had indeed very little in the way of documents on which to rely, and anyway chronological accuracy never worried him particularly. Hence the fact that these autobiographical works have often proved a snare to subsequent biographers of the author.

The form which Strindberg adopted for the series was dictated by the view of literature which he held during these years 1885–6; commenting on the Naturalist novel in 1885, he had prophesied: 'Authorship will gradually cease. Future generations ought to set up offices in which every person, at a certain age, should hand in a truthful biography, which could provide material for a real science of human beings, if such were to be needed.'[1] On the ground, then, that the only person whom an author can really know and accurately dissect, is himself,

[1] See document quoted by Birger Mörner in *Den Strindberg jag känt* (1924), p. 167.

Strindberg set out to reveal himself, through what he described as 'an experiment in the literature of the future', in a deliberately 'unconstructed' narrative. Seemingly formless and artless *The Son of the Bondwoman* is; actually considerable technical skill is implicit in the interweaving of personal events, and contemporary political, sociological, and literary developments, with the psychological analysis, in which lies the chief interest of the series.

For where, as Strindberg pointed out, Zola, in his Naturalist novels, had emphasised the importance of physiological factors, Strindberg lays stress on the psychological, when he brings into his account the physical and physiological 'circumstances' which shape the development of Johan; for instance, the tendencies inherited from his parents and absorbed from his wet-nurse, the economic distress and subsequent recovery of his father, the conditions at the various schools he attended, and so on. Especially in the first two volumes, *The Son of the Bondwoman* and *The Time of Ferment (Jäs-ningstiden)*, do these factors receive emphasis. Inspired by his then dominant belief that literature should be utilitarian, not aesthetic, in intention, Strindberg looked upon his work as scientific.

This, to be sure, strikes one as an unjustified pretension. Writing as he does of events which had taken place, in some cases, thirty or thirty-five years before, and of which he had only the most shadowy personal memory, he builds up these recollections with the power and vitality of his mature imagination, and considers the reactions and emotions of his childhood and adolescence from the point of view of the complex and frustrated author of thirty-seven. His portrayal of his student life in Uppsala and of his tutorships in Stockholm is also no doubt coloured by subsequent experiences; Strindberg's fluidity in changing his opinions was such that even incidents dating back merely a few years had probably taken on quite a different significance by the time he reported them in *In the Red Room* and *The Author*. Yet more intensely subjective though they are—probably for that very reason—the first two volumes are far more fascinating than the two subsequent books.

Strindberg may not have been so unhappy a child as he pictured himself in *The Son of the Bondwoman*, but, morbidly sensitive as he certainly was from his early childhood (as is indicated by independent family testimony), it must have been difficult for him not to be unhappy, given the circumstances of his family life. Afraid, under-nourished, pushed about on all sides, and uncertain of affection, as he struggled for a place in the over-crowded home opposite Klarakyrkan in rivalry with his tougher brothers and sisters, Johan or August presents the perfect text-book case for the child-guidance clinic of our days. When one has wandered about in the Stockholm of to-day, in the narrow streets surrounding the dark and dreary churchyard of St Clara, and has envisaged the kind of life led by the Strindberg family in the 1850's, one sympathises more readily with the self-pity which Strindberg felt only too intensely. This narrow, gloomy, paternal tyranny and ineffective maternal affection remind one curiously of Hebbel's *Maria Magdalena* and the household of Meister Anton. In the latter work the family are all petty bourgeois; in Strindberg's family the strains were conflicting, the father being middle-class and the mother of much humbler origin, a former servant-girl and waitress. Hence the doubt in Strindberg's mind as to where he really belonged, in the kitchen with the servants, or at the elegant table of the prosperous, cultivated doctor in Stockholm (Axel Lamm), who took him on as tutor to his children in 1868, after his frustrations at Uppsala, and treated him as one of his family. The intensity of Strindberg's consciousness of this dualism in himself, which runs through the volumes as their *leit-motif*, is reflected in the very choice of title for the whole series, *The Son of the Bondwoman*. With a kind of self-tormenting irony typical of himself Strindberg exposes his lowly origins to his reading public. It is, of course, possible that he exaggerated this shameful awareness of his lower-class streak, when he came to interpret the feelings of his childhood and youth; but, on the other hand, such a consciousness of inferiority, as revealed in shabby clothing and cheap lodgings, is, as everyone knows, particularly painful to school-children and adolescents. When the fortunes of the Strindberg family improved, and Johan lived in better surroundings, and mingled with the aristocratic youths at the Stockholm Lyceum, he enjoyed the amelioration in his position, but was tormented by the feeling that he must not deny his other side. It seems probable that his persistent and uneasy consciousness of 'What will people say?' which, explicitly or implicitly, lies behind so many of his actions and speeches throughout his life, his revolts *pour épater les bourgeois* and his sudden panicky withdrawals, can be explained by the fact of his origin as 'the bondwoman's son'.

Yet, considering this dualism again, one is tempted to wonder whether Strindberg's explanation of the conflict within him is not really just a convenient projection, and whether the cause of his maladjustment to life did not lie deeper still, namely in that curious instability of character of which all his life appears to be a reflection, a morbid reaction against *tryck*, or pressure, in any form.

Certainly the tug-of-war between his upper-class and lower-class sympathies explains the changes in his political views. An amusing incident—amusing, that is, for the reader—is described in *The Time of Ferment*. Johan is accompanying his charges on a journey to Denmark, and on the boat they encounter a roughish lot of small tradesmen, grocers, sweeps, etc. who behave aggressively towards the youths. Johan feels himself insulted on behalf of his charges. Liberal at first, then Socialist, finally a kind of aristocrat, he proclaims his belief in a new anarchy, and ends his fourth volume, *The Author*, with an account of a conversation with X (that is, the Swedish poet and nobleman Heidenstam, with whom he had discussed these problems at Schloss Brunegg in Switzerland). Here X or Heidenstam states his belief in the inevitable struggle for power between the different classes of society, which must be viewed without any sentimental idealism, and Strindberg outlines a kind of 'private socialism', stripped of all *pjåsk*, or sentimental fuss (a term which now includes the Christian or any other theistic doctrines), in which the stronger beings will rise free of the chains of mediocrity.

The conversations with the elegant, arrogant, and financially independent young Heidenstam must have had a Romantic quality of their own—with the ancient but draughty halls of Brunegg as setting. The adjective Romantic is often drawn from the reader by Strindberg's reactions in these would-be Naturalist volumes; see for instance the description, in *The Time of Ferment*, of Johan's behaviour at the demonstrations which took place in front of the new statue of Charles XII in Stockholm. 'And there they came marching, the blue guardsmen, the foundations of society, on which those above supported themselves. Johan was seized by a wild desire to go against this mass of horses, human beings, sabres, as if in these he had seen all that pressure embodied. It was the enemy; right, then, he would encounter it. The troop advances, and Johan takes up his position in the middle of the street.'[1] But the would-be Romantic hero does not fulfil himself in action; a kind observer pushes him out of the way, and he is accompanied back to the doctor's house, safe from any danger.

In the descriptions of Johan's amours, in such episodes as when Johan rushes out into the woods after having unintentionally insulted his beloved, a waitress at Stallmästaregården, one finds humour, but often, too, a kind of exaggerated morbid eroticism may be observed. One is reminded of passages in that Romantic novel, Sainte-Beuve's *Volupté*, in which the author most skilfully describes Amaury's scenes with Madame R., whom the hero would like to make his mistress. 'Je disais tout cela en paroles sèches, sifflantes, articulées, frappant du doigt, comme en mesure, sa plus belle boule favorite d'hortensia, d'où tombait à chaque coup une nuée de parcelles détachées. Elle m'écoutait debout, croisant les bras, pâle, violette et muette, dans un long sarrau gris du matin. Mais, indigné de cet impassible silence, et m'excitant au son de ma colère, je m'approchai d'elle; j'étendis la main et je l'enfonçai avec fureur dans la chevelure négligée qui s'assemblait derrière sa tête, la tenant ainsi sous ma prise et continuant à sa face ma lente invective....'

The common source for these attitudes, which often occur in relation to non-erotic objects, is probably Rousseau. Strindberg, to do him justice, realised his own Romantic tendencies, and refers to them on several occasions in the autobiography, for instance in *The Time*

[1] *S.S.* XVIII, 297–8.

of Ferment: 'In Johan, who was a Romantic, lay the will to step forward and speak to the people',[1] and so on.

In other passages, however, Johan's feelings for the other sex appear of the most simple physical nature, and these relationships with prostitutes—they can hardly be described as amours—are frequently referred to before his marriage; see for instance the account of the Runa Literary Society's picnic and its ending (Chapter 8 in *The Time of Ferment*).

Behind all Strindberg's relations with women, sooner or later, in varying degree, and beginning with his mother, appears his hatred for the sex as a whole. In the first volumes, written soon after the *Married* crisis, this hatred makes itself especially noticeable, so that the criticism of his dead mother, voiced in 1866, can be directly attributed to the effect upon him of what he called 'the international women's league'. This hatred of women was to find a more neurotic expression in *A Madman's Defence* (*Le Plaidoyer d'un Fou* or *En Dåres Försvarstal*), his next essay in autobiography. These analyses of relationships and dissections of himself provide what might be called the Naturalist apparatus in the work, and furnish fascinating material on Strindberg's state of mind. Revealing remarks are scattered broadcast throughout the text, as when he writes: 'The whole is a mixture of modesty and impudence characteristic of the man'[2] (i.e. Johan). And, however Romantic the attitude depicted, the language used is restrained and almost casual; an attempt at suicide may be followed by the account of a meal, and both be given equal emphasis. For this an extreme detachment might be responsible, but after a while it becomes difficult not to believe that Strindberg, in some ways, really has quite

[1] *S.S.* xviii, 310.   [2] *S.S.* xviii, 364.

a different sense from that of most people, as to what is important and what is not. This may be connected, mentally, with the quality which he called 'karaktärs-löshet' (lack of defined character), and on which he prided himself, vaunting his own capacity for changing his points of view, as proof of his innate originality. Perhaps this helps to explain the strange planlessness of his existence, to which *The Son of the Bondwoman* testifies so vividly. Johan's course from Stockholm to Uppsala and back again, the retreats from one career to another, teacher, doctor, actor, telegraphist, and so on, strike one as quite peculiarly aimless. In this respect, as in so many others, *The Son of the Bondwoman* contains a great deal of material on Strindberg's psyche that is valuable not just for what is said by the author, but for the way he says it. Often, indeed, the omissions of the bond-woman's son are as significant as his admissions.

In *A Madman's Defence* (which was written in French, but first appeared in a pirated German edition in 1893) Strindberg treats that section of his life—his relation-ship with Siri von Essen—which had been left decently veiled in the preceding autobiographical works. It was actually written in 1887–8, while he was still married to Siri von Essen, and even contains some of the original letters which had passed between them in 1875–6, and which, with others, were printed under the title *Han och Hon* (*He and She*) in 1919. No other work of Strindberg's breathes quite such a vehement hatred for women as does this. 'Utterly caddish' might well have been, probably was, the comment provoked in the literary salons of the 'nineties on the author of these revelations of pre-nuptial joys and matrimonial torments. Strindberg intended the book as an indict-ment of his wife, a defence of his own sanity against the conspiracy led by his wife to immure him in an asylum. In reality the work has served certain psycho-analysts as proof of Strindberg's madness, providing, in their view, evidence of schizophrenia, or else of persecution mania.[1] Without considering here whether Strindberg was sane or insane at the time he wrote *A Madman's Defence*, one may observe that as a defence of the author's own behaviour the book fails, in that the brutality and self-righteousness he displays in many passages are bound to set the reader against him. Unfaithfulness, sexual perversion, drunkenness, are some of the practices with which he charges his wife (here rechristened Maria), not to mention irresponsibility and dishonesty in financial affairs. It must be accepted that Strindberg really believed in the facts as he put them down, and that unconsciously he twisted words and incidents from his memories into indictments against Siri, with all the suspicious mentality characteristic of persecution-mania or incipient persecution-mania. He starts from the time when Siri was still the Baron's wife, and brings the account up to the time of writing, when he proposes that she shall stay with him while the divorce is carried through, and live with him as his mistress.

After he had completed this book, Strindberg realised that it was scandalous. The first words in the Preface admit this: 'This is a horrible book.'[2] The last words in it are addressed to his wife: 'The story is now concluded, my beloved. I have avenged myself; we are quits.'[3] It was characteristic of Strindberg that after a literary paying of scores of this kind he should still be capable of loving Siri, and of making yet another start

---

[1] See for instance Jaspers, K., *Strindberg und Van Gogh* (1922) and pp. 61 ff. above.

[2] *S.S.* xxvi, 5.   [3] *S.S.* xxvi, 377.

with her—and even more typical that he should expect her to be patient and forbearing enough to co-operate. Only the most deep-rooted insecurity, utter dependence on feminine tenderness and physical response, and the accompanying and equally intense resentment at this dependence can explain, and to some degree excuse, what is Strindberg's most repellent and also most tragic work.

From the literary standpoint Strindberg handles his material skilfully. The book is written in the first person, and succeeds in compelling the reader's interest. It contains, too, some very attractive descriptions of the relationship between Siri and Strindberg, when they were both at their happiest: spring and summer scenes in Sweden and the Alps, with bird-song and flowers and music. Other passages, analyses of regrets and desires, recall again the attitudinising in that *genre* of Romantic novel of which *Volupté* is an interesting specimen, and against which Flaubert warns so subtly in *Madame Bovary*. Strindberg, who, as already noted, was familiar with Flaubert, in one passage actually warns Maria, then in Copenhagen, against becoming a Madame Bovary, but he does not apply his discernment to himself.

Yet certain passages, especially, of course, when one reads them in the French version, strike one almost as parodies of Flaubert's masterpiece. So, for example: 'Sous les voûtes ogivales des sapins, où la brise psalmodiait parmi les branches à aiguilles, la détresse m'angoissa de plus belle. C'était ici que nous nous promenions lorsque le soleil printanier brillait dans les verdures, quand les sapins poussaient leurs fleurs pourprées qui fleurent le parfum de fraise, quand le genévrier jetait sa poussière jaune au vent, quand les anémones perçaient les feuilles mortes dessous les coudriers. C'était ici, sur cette mousse brune, molle ainsi qu'une couverture de laine, que trottinaient ses petits pieds tandis que d'une voix timbrée elle chantait ses chansons finlandaises.'[1]

By the time Strindberg had finished *The Son of the Bondwoman*, he had realised that scientific writing did not satisfy him, and had returned to *belles lettres*. The years 1887 and 1888 form a particularly productive period in his life as an author. The next autobiographical works to be considered, *Inferno* and *Legends* (*Legender*), first written in French, mark the beginning of that new creative period, following on a period of sterility, which brought forth *To Damascus* and the historical dramas, discussed above in Chapter V. In fact *Inferno* and *Legends* appear as crystallisations of the conflicting ideas and sentiments associated with Strindberg's so-called 'Inferno Crisis'.[2] Their chief interest lies in the reporting, with comment, of the experiences Strindberg went through in Austria, France, and the South of Sweden, experiences for which he himself often adduced a supernatural interpretation, but which, for the reader of these volumes, are more convincingly explained in psychological and psychopathological terms. As in this connection they have already been discussed above (see Chapter III, sections 3 and 5), there is no need to dwell on them here. The fact that, against the supra-natural theories which the author proffers, the common-sense explanation, unbidden, so constantly springs to the mind—and in this respect these works are unlike the other autobiographical writings, in which the reader's critical sense is often lulled by the author's powers—lessens both their human and their literary appeal. The form, the detailed jotting down of trivial incidents, detracts from their value;

---

[1] *Le Plaidoyer d'un Fou* (revised French version, Paris, 1895), pp. 141–2.
[2] See above, Chapter III.

actually the two books contain extracts from Strindberg's contemporary diaries, but these were so abridged in form that the later writing-up of these items has really changed their significance. They are not, then, nor is the rest, a scientific recording of daily observations, but incidents recalled and interpreted imaginatively and fantastically, some time after they had taken place. They have not, therefore, the value of clinical casebooks, though many of the trivialities cited, the bad coffee, the piano-playing, and so on, recall the pettiness of some scientific logbooks. Indeed, their pseudoscientific character supplies a further clue to Strindberg's mentality in these years of crisis up to the final settling in Lund. Thus it is impossible fully to understand Strindberg's state of mind without reading these works, and yet the paradox, that they also mislead a reader, is almost equally valid. Possibly it is the frankly childish nature of many of the phenomena which puts one off—we have most of us, when children, gone through the stage of jumping in the squares, withheld by primitive fears from treading on the lines; and it may be that, having advanced beyond this primitive stage of fear, we are reluctant to confess to any other such lingering superstitions and resentful of a writer who insists on dragging out these naïve and yet fantastic fears and beliefs into the light of day. By writing *Inferno* and *Legends*, Strindberg certainly rid his system of some of the worst of his horrors, and found his way to renewed literary activity. Bald though most of *Inferno* and the first part of *Legends* are in style, the fragment *Jacob Wrestling* (*Jakob brottas*) in *Legends*, in which, among other things, Strindberg describes the visions he had of Christ by the Luxembourg Gardens, reaches a much higher literary standard. One feels in reading it that

Strindberg's poetic imagination has quickened again, evocative now not only of spiritual struggles for salvation, but also of the atmosphere of the quiet grey streets of the Cité, and the budding avenues in the Luxembourg Gardens. On these vivid sense-impressions Strindberg was to draw later for his new poetic dramas.

The little volume *Alone* (*Ensam*), the last of the autobiographical works to be considered here, appeared in the autumn of 1903, but was actually completed in June of that year, while Harriet and Anne-Marie were still with Strindberg. The title indicates the change which was taking place at the time in Strindberg's life. The marriage with Harriet was on the point of failing, though it was not finally dissolved until the following year, and Strindberg again felt both alone and lonely: the Swedish word *ensam* expresses both these things. Of all Strindberg's autobiographical writings it is surely the most attractive, breathing a gentler melancholy, a quieter resignation, than he had ever known or expressed. This mood resembles that in *The Storm*, the Chamber Play which portrays the life of the old man alone in his Stockholm flat. Here, with a far-sightedness not otherwise characteristic of him, Strindberg is taking stock of those inward resources which will have to bear him along when his family have actually left him. Harriet Bosse's professional activities and absences had already given him a foretaste of the solitude to come.

Thus *Alone* is not a factual narrative of Strindberg's life in 1903. In it he already refers to himself as a widower, and describes excursions to cafés where, with the friends of his youth, he attempts to pick up old threads, being now justified in leading such a life again. But the old relationships will not revive; too much has happened, on both sides, in the interval; old words have taken on new meanings, and are greeted with suspicion. So he withdraws to his own rooms in Karlavägen, and there learns, as he says, 'to hear the silence and listen to the new voices audible in it'.[1] The values which he discovers and rediscovers in this way are in his books: books of devotion, from the Bible to Buddhist meditations, then Goethe, Schiller, Balzac, and so on, his reading matter being dictated by his moods, which also determine his choice of walks in Stockholm. When he felt particularly black, he would follow what he called his *via dolorosa*, and, wandering through the narrow alleys and avenues that overlooked the Castle, or the Old Town, would sink back into memories aroused by the houses he saw. Here he had played as a child, this way he had rushed unwillingly to school, here at this corner was the registrar's office where he had arranged for his banns a long time ago. The past mingles with the present, and the Stockholm of fifty years earlier, with its orchards and farmhouses, rises as clear before his eyes as the modern capital. The feeling of loneliness was sometimes so intense, in spite of work and books, that he felt as if he were buried alive, and one evening he fled on to a tram, merely in order to hear human voices, and be comforted by the pressure of a stranger's elbow against his side. To escape his loneliness, he made up stories about the people whom he used to meet on his morning walks, the retired major, the elderly lady with two dogs, who always aroused Swedenborgian thoughts (for Strindberg hated dogs) on the enforced company of animals as a punishment for misanthropy, the little old woman who appeared mysteriously now and again, and to whose comings and goings he attributed an occult significance. This circle of acquaintances included, too,

[1] *S.S.* xxxviii, 127.

the other tenants in his house, whom he observed and about whose lot he speculated—the piano players, the dog owners, whose summer absences left such long silences in the apartment house. Strindberg captures subtly the rhythm of life in the city, and its spring freshness, its winter heaviness, are sketched in charming vignettes.

Driven in as he is upon himself, he finds that the smells, the sounds, above all the sights around him have to serve as stimulants for his creative faculties, and, with his curious facility for dramatising a *rencontre* or a street incident, he writes it down as the basis for a play. Even the sight from the street of a lighted window, with a family gathered together round a table, a party of card-players, or just a young woman with a child, sets his imagination working; and, as evidence of his particular method of dramatic conception, *Alone* offers most interesting matter. Strindberg sympathises with the sufferings of these strangers, takes pleasure in their joys, then returns home to his solitude and work. The solitude was to continue for the rest of his days, the gentle resignation, unfortunately, did not last.

CHAPTER IX

MISCELLANEOUS WORKS

CLEARLY only a small section of the so far unclassified writings remaining In the fifty-five volumes of Strindberg's collected works can be considered in this chapter; given the purpose of this book, only a limited selection would, in any case, be desirable. No attempt will be made, for example, to discuss the scientific or pseudo-scientific work such as *Anti-Barbarus* or the specifically philological studies, but those writings to be included here will as far as possible be grouped according to their subject-matter: the first group to be examined will consist of those works which are concerned with *kultur-historia,* that is, the history of civilization.

The satire *The New State* (*Det Nya Riket*), of 1882, may be called a negative contribution to this subject, in that therein Strindberg castigated all those aspects of contemporary Swedish society which he particularly hated. The quotation, on the title-page, from *Pickwick Papers*—'You are a humbug, sir...'—is, so to speak, the *leit-motif* of the ten chapters, each of which is aimed at a contemporary institution or set of people, each exposing a racket in the same way as *The Red Room* set out to unmask a series of frauds. But the satire in *The New State* is bitterer and more mordant both in spirit and expression. Indeed, Strindberg never achieved a more controlled mastery of the medium than in this book, for he does not here, as so often, lapse into the merely grotesque, a fact which explains why the satire has retained its interest.

Strindberg had, indeed, a fruitful subject, for the Sweden of the early 1880's seemed to him, and not only to him, sunk in apathy after the constitutional reforms of 1866; the reforms of the franchise of that year were in his eyes mere valueless compromises wrung from the unwilling monarchy and government. The vision of a new era of liberal reconstruction that had hovered before the eyes of at least some idealists had been eclipsed by the plans for economic exploitation launched by the punch-drinking, cigar-smoking new capitalists who provoked much of Strindberg's most trenchant satire. Meanwhile the Royal Academy, the Royal Theatre, and similar institutions, continued to venerate the conventions of the past, and woe betide anyone who attempted to throw open a window in these shrines and let in a little fresh air. In the chapter *A National Educational Institution* (*En Nationell Bildningsanstalt*) Strindberg first describes the manager's afternoon reception in his office at the Royal Theatre, at which he deals ruthlessly with complaints: 'The secretary sat by the door in the anteroom and knew whom he should let in. The others were told that the manager had so much to do that they had better return on Friday. This information was regularly passed to all the dramatists who did not belong to the Chancellery of the National Theatre, all the beginners, and in addition all those who had a salary of less than 2000 crowns. The Marquise (that is, the actress taking that part) was admitted first, as her business was the most important. The Manager: "The first act, a mauve satin dress with a train six yards long." "Eight, if you please, the duchess's was seven yards in *Cocotte or Coquette*."[1]' And so on.

The description of the visit to the theatre paid by a

[1] *S.S.* x, 133–4.

country M.P. and his family forms the second part of this chapter, in which the parodies speak for themselves and require no comment by the author. One chapter is devoted to the Jews, another to the Upper House, part of this being in the form of a lively narrative by a bug from the Press Gallery bench. Many of the personages are modelled closely on living contemporaries, whom Strindberg knew and hated, hated in many cases because they had ventured to criticize his own works. C. D. af Wirsén, the critic and poet, Warburg and Schück the literary historians, Eichhorn, Strindberg's colleague in the Royal Library, could all recognise themselves in these malicious portraits.

The hero, to whom the book is dedicated, is the Swedish people, exploited, fussed over, and made a fool of by humbugging institutions and organisations, and particularly the country people, whom Strindberg, at this time full of Rousseauistic enthusiasm for the peasantry, was eager to defend. This fact links the book with Strindberg's preceding, positive work on the history of civilisation, *The Swedish People on Holy Days and Working Days* (*Det Svenska Folket i Hälg och Söcken*); in fact, the bad reception which this earlier work had received largely called forth Strindberg's polemics in *The New State*; not the least remarkable feature of *The New State* is that, with such a personal inspiration for the bitterness, the satire should be maintained on so uniform a level.

With *The Swedish People* Strindberg had set out to expose the falsity of the history written by Geijer and his followers, who were concerned to glorify the deeds and importance of the Swedish kings. Instead, he describes the work and play of the ordinary Swedish citizens, thanks to whose efforts and patience the kings were enabled to rule. He tackled his task armed with the results of a good deal of scholarly research, and with poetic imagination as well, so that the work when completed offered a strange but interesting combination of facts and hypotheses covering the period from the 9th century A.D. up to 1865.

As the work occupies only two volumes, obviously a great many things must have been omitted, and indeed Strindberg confessed as much in his postscript, writing that he had believed it possible to have room in the space at his disposal, limited though it was from the start, for a Swedish history of civilisation, but had found in the course of the work that he must confine himself to a sketch for such a work, which, as a result, now contained partly too much, partly too little.[1] However, Strindberg has succeeded, even if some of the material in certain chapters is inadequately presented and the whole is too superficial, in producing a lively and vivid account, illustrated by quotations from chronicles and contemporary letters, especially of the Middle Ages and the sixteenth century. He uses, among others, the device of describing journeys inside the country or along the coasts, to give movement to his text. The most striking feature of *The Swedish People* is the evidence it provides as to Strindberg's conception of history, a much wider conception than that prevailing among most contemporary historians in Scandinavia. Strindberg grasped the interaction of the social, economic, political, and ideological factors in the life of a country, and, even if he failed to achieve his object of portraying that complicated network, he did at least bring a much more imaginative approach to his subject than did those whom he called 'pedants'.

[1] *S.S.* VIII, 456–7.

Strindberg used the work as a vehicle for certain polemical ideas, many of which he emphasised again in *The New State*, primarily, as stated above, in order to discredit Geijer's views on history, but also to champion the people, and more especially the rights of the agricultural population, to the point of maintaining, like Rousseau, that society was merely artificial; that the Jews in Sweden lived a parasitical existence; and that women should be respected as wives and mothers, and allowed independent activity, but in no circumstances idolised as superior beings. These provocative views, together with the sins against historical accuracy, explain the unfavourable reception of *The Swedish People* when it appeared.

An earlier work, with a much more limited canvas, *Old Stockholm (Gamla Stockholm)*, published 1880-2, had been well received, partly, no doubt, because his collaborator, Claes Lundin, through his standard of scholarship, had forced Strindberg to revise his own: it should, however, be stressed that the inspiration for the work, and its conception, came from Strindberg. He did so reconsider his own scholarly standards without modifying his natural enthusiasm for his subject; his love of Stockholm, after all, continued to be one of the great passions of his life, till the end of his days. All Strindberg's appreciation of 'things' (to which Rilke, notably, gave a more mystical but also more pretentious expression), and his interest in technique as such, which are revealed for instance in the best passages of *The People of Hemsö*, come to the fore in these descriptions of Stockholm and its customs.

The variety of Strindberg's interests and his knowledge of the history of civilisation are shown by his range of subject-matter. In *Studies in the History of Civilisation*

(*Kulturhistoriska Studier*) he gives, among other things, an account of the work of Swedish explorers and missionaries in Asia, and discusses the Chinese language; in *Among French Peasants* (*Bland Franska Bönder*), written five years after the publication of the above (i.e. in 1886) the details of life among this section of the French population are studied, with a quick eye for local peculiarities. The main problem raised for Strindberg by this journey in France was that of the agricultural crisis and its repercussions on the peasantry. His discussion of this problem, and the solutions he proposes, were coloured by his belief in Rousseau and by other more modern socialists' demands for socialisation of the land. Yet this faith in nature, Rousseau, and the peasantry, was already waning. Political factors, rather than economic, occupied his attention, and already in the essays *Concerning the General Discontent* (*Om det allmänna Missnöjet*) and *The Over-valuation of Cultural Work* (*Kulturarbetets Överskattning*),[1] wherein he demonstrated to his own satisfaction the futility of most of the professions followed in 'society', for example, that of the monarch, the doctor, and so on, and of society's institutions, Strindberg's anarchistic impulses, rather than any belief in progress, assert themselves. One of the logical conclusions from this point of view was Strindberg's disparagement of his own profession, and this, as has been noted above in Chapter VIII, led him at one point to abandon *belles lettres* entirely in favour of journalism, though not for long. By one of those violent swings of the pendulum, of which Strindberg's life offers several examples, the press articles which he wrote during the last years of his life[2] again championed the cause of the

[1] Both published in *One Thing and Another* (*Likt och Olikt*), 1884, *S.S.* XVI. [2] See *S.S.* LIII *passim*.

agricultural workers and their rights to the land, taking up also the plight of the urban proletariat. The increasing influence exerted by the Conservatives after 1906 no doubt partly explains this reversion to his early standpoint; Strindberg's instinct to belong to the Opposition continued vigorous to the end.

For such a prolific author as Strindberg, the amount of literary criticism in his writings is small, that is, of 'pure' literary criticism, for comments on literary topics often occur in essays on historical and sociological subjects. Strindberg's absorption in these aspects of life explains his reluctance to dwell on analysis of form and similar problems; his violent personal prejudices often cause his writings about other authors to take the shape of personal attacks, and lessen the permanent value and interest of what he had to say.

So he assailed the poetry of the 'Pseudonym poets', whose graceful yet conventional regrets and joys (he considered) vitiated contemporary taste, in that they perpetuated what one might call 'epigone-romanticism' in an age which dreaded realism, and also because they looked to his critic and butt, Wirsén, as their arbiter and king. Behind his bitter onslaughts, especially on Heidenstam and Levertin, after 1890, and on their attempts to move literature away from the factory and the workshops, lay doubtless a personal feeling of jealousy, because these poets had stolen a march on him, but also a genuine disapproval of their mannered styles and their cult of the aristocratic.

In Strindberg's reviews of earlier Swedish literature, the popular Bellman figures as chief bugbear. In the frivolity of this elegant tippler poet of the eighteenth century, Strindberg fastened on something which always eluded him in his own writing, the apparently insouciant acceptance of the sordidness of life, free from resentment or reforming zeal. Critical comments on Bellman, and others, occur in the autobiographies, and in the series of newspaper articles published in *Speeches to the Swedish Nation* (*Tal till Svenska Nationen*), *The Popular State* (*Folkstaten*), and *Religious Renascence* (*Religiös Renässans*) in 1910. Tegnér, in spite of the fact that Heidenstam, too, admired him, Strindberg continued to praise; he lauded also Bjørnson, but not Ibsen.

Of the literary criticism, the writings on the drama, as might have been expected, retain the greatest interest, though even in this field Strindberg produced surprisingly little 'pure' criticism. The Preface to *Lady Julia* has already been considered in Chapter V; it had for Strindberg himself the significance of a manifesto in favour of his own Naturalist or semi-Naturalist plays. Apart from the multiplicity of the motives, the characterlessness of the personages, the abolition of curtain-drops, and the development of a free dialogue, with the use, too, of mime, Strindberg claimed that he had demonstrated, by his staging of the play, the value of retaining one setting throughout, simply and realistically equipped (as a protest against the extravagance of the accepted fashion); he urged, too, that footlights be done away with, and a subtler method of lighting from the sides, together with a less stylised use of make-up, be introduced. All these innovations—really a means of creating a more convincing illusion of reality on the stage—have long since ceased to appear unusual. Strindberg would, however, no doubt find much to criticise in the theatre of today, even if the vexatious habit of occupiers of an *oxöga* (bull's eye box) supping during the performance has died out.

In the later essay *Concerning the Modern Drama and*

the Modern Stage (*Om Modernt Drama och Modern Teater*)
Strindberg carries the observations made in the Preface
a step further: he advocates the playing of *quarts
d'heure*, as they were called at the Théâtre Libre in
Paris, brief one-acters, containing only the *scène à faire*
from the potential three- or five-act dramas which
might be built around that kernel. Why, argues Strindberg, weary audience, actors, and producers with the
other scenes, when the interest is anyway concentrated in this one? That is to say, Strindberg praises
the psychological drama, connecting it historically with
the drama of the Greeks, at the expense of the
play of intrigue, and in doing so he pays tribute,
for various services rendered, to Molière, Racine, and
Zola. In the novels of Zola he finds the necessary
discrimination between photographic realism, which does
not see the wood for the trees, and 'great naturalism',
which depicts the conflicts between the forces of
nature, 'which finds beautiful or ugly a matter of
indifference, so long as it is great'. These observations,
written as they were in 1889, that is, not very long
before *In the Outer Skerries*, with its curious compound
of naturalism and aestheticism, serve as a definition of
what he attempted in his own one-act plays, *Pariah,
Simoom*, etc.

The *Open Letters to the Intimate Theatre* (*Öppna Brev till
Intima Teatern*), which, as published in the Collected
Works, contain not only these letters themselves, but
also a memorandum, and various essays on certain of
Shakespeare's plays, were occasioned by Strindberg's
practical concern with problems of stagecraft at the
Intimate Theatre, and date from the years 1908–9.
The mingling in them of comments on modern stage
technique, criticisms of rival companies, and analyses of

Shakespeare and Goethe, produces a blend peculiar to Strindberg in its freshness, concision, and lack of inner logical connection. Considering the lapse in time and the changes in Strindberg's own dramatic style, since he wrote the Preface to *Lady Julia*, one might perhaps expect to find considerable transformations of the writer's theories; but, if so, one would be disappointed. It is true that Strindberg has reduced some of his claims for a realistic presentation on the stage; nevertheless he still wishes the actor to strive for a natural, easy style, while giving full value to the language, a freedom which, as he puts it, is achieved only through perfect control of body and mind. In Shakespeare it is still the realism of tone he admires, that is, the juxtaposition of comic and tragic scenes which had appealed to his imagination so many years ago, but he criticises Shakespeare as well, on all manner of minor points. His attempts to prove that Shakespeare is an orthodox Christian, and also a woman-hater, become, at times, undeniably fanciful, but no more so than a great deal of scholarly Shakespearean criticism. Strindberg's preoccupation with moral issues strikes one especially in these discussions of Shakespeare.

With regard to technical aspects of the drama, Strindberg's comments on the productions of his own plays at the Intimate Theatre are of particular interest. As a result of lack of both space and money, apart from any theories of art, the staging at Norra Bantorget tended towards simplicity, and effects were increasingly obtained by experiments with the lighting, against backgrounds of heavy velvets. Strindberg personally urged this device on Falck, and in the latter's book[1] there is an amusing description of a stage party at the

[1] August Falck, *Fem År med Strindberg* (Stockholm, 1935).

Intimate Theatre, at which Strindberg, with cries of
'more light, more light!' persuaded the members of the
party to move the draperies from behind, while various
coloured lights were trained in such a way as to ripple
over the surface. Here Strindberg was anticipating
modern developments, but he does not really expatiate
on the technique of the future in these notes, and it is
doubtful whether he himself realised the possibilities
in respect of stagecraft which his post-Inferno plays, in
particular, offer. Indeed, while he was anxious to point
out that certain apparent obstacles to production could
be overcome in this way, his own taste still remained
limited by the conventions of the period—by that
Edwardian ornamentation and fussiness which surround
him in the photographs of his flats, and which make
it at times difficult to accept him as the prophet of
streamlined austerity in the theatre.

Ideally speaking, the poetry of Strindberg should
have had a chapter, or at least a complete subsection of
a chapter, to itself; but for the purposes of this book
it will be dealt with briefly. For, since all quotations
here must be given in English, and since very little of
Strindberg's poetry has been translated, and that not to
great advantage, it is disproportionately difficult to do
justice to the lyrics. Strindberg's vitality as a lyric poet
derives largely from his use of language, just as, when
writing in prose, he handles words vigorously and with an
individual boldness; for he is not afraid to introduce the
most idiomatic expressions and forthright words, drawing
always on his very extensive vocabulary both of modern
technical and of older country terms. The temptation,
therefore, to reduce the verses to a more conventional
poetic formula, in translation, becomes particularly
dangerous when dealing with Strindberg.

That several of his dramas, notably *The Dream Play*, contain scenes or interludes in verse, has already been mentioned. In fact, the bulk of his lyrical poetry is small, consisting of the collection *Poems in Verse and Prose* (*Dikter på Vers och Prosa*) of 1883, *Somnambulistic Nights by Broad Daylight* (*Sömngångarnätter på Vakna Dagar*), of the following year, and *Word Play and Minor Art* (*Ordalek och Småkonst*), an expansion published in 1905 of the verses printed in the volume *Fagervik and Skamsund*, including among others also one of Strindberg's finest, *Ahasverus*, on the theme of the Wandering Jew; a few others were published after his death. Even these lyrical poems often verge on dramatic verse, just as some of the best passages in his verse plays have a lyric tone, for instance the Song of the Winds in *The Dream Play*, in which Strindberg achieves some of his finest musical effects.

Strindberg's first collection (in which he included also earlier poems reshaped) was intended as a challenge to the Naturalistic School and its assumption that all literature must be prose. By writing poetry at all, and by writing it in such language, he shocked all sections of literary opinion. Several of the poems have a polemical intention, for example, *An Idealist's Criticism* (*Idealistkritik*) and *For Freedom of Thought* (*För Tankens Frihet*), and show Heine's influence; others, such as the charming *Sun Smoke* (*Solrök*), which celebrates his meeting with Siri, are based on personal emotions. In *Somnambulistic Nights* (mostly written in Paris) Strindberg carries on the process of liberation which he began in certain of the *Poems*, and rejects the conventions of the contemporary Swedish lyric by employing *Knittelvers*, or rhymed doggerel verse. He rightly considered later that with this volume he had pointed out the way to Heidenstam and the other Swedish lyric poets of the 'nineties, in extending the boundaries of verse. He used his freedom to attack the aesthetic ideals of antiquity, and the slavish worship of science, and also to express his longing for the skerries.

In *Word Play*, another work inspired by the relationship with Harriet Bosse, and in this sense, too, akin to the deeply lyrical *Crown Bride*, Strindberg somewhat paradoxically combines the classical hexameter with free verse. Thus, *The Journey to Town (Stadsresan)*, the description of a sexton's adventures, follows, in a manner all Strindberg's own, the classical pattern, and also evokes with most attractive freshness the atmosphere of a midsummer day in the Stockholm skerries. In *Trinity Eve (Trefaldighetsnatten)* the hexameter is varied by interpolations in other metres from some of the characters, and the poet (Skalden) contributes the changing *Crysdëtos* cycle, perhaps the most haunting of Strindberg's lyrics, in its fusion of symbolical—almost surrealist—images and sound effects. Very seldom does Strindberg, as a lyric poet, achieve the seemingly effortless musical power of his great contemporary Fröding; he is often careless, even awkward, but his best work is carried along by a kind of nervous vigour.

Last of the works to be mentioned in this chapter, and defying all attempts at classification by subject-matter, comes *A Blue Book (En Blå Bok)*, 1907, which, with its three companion volumes, of which the last came out posthumously in 1912, forms a sort of 'omnium gatherum' of Strindberg's ideas on religion, philosophy, occultism, philology, literature, science, and so on. In a sense they are books of essays; in fact the first volume, dedicated to Swedenborg, is divided into page-long discourses, most of them beginning: 'The teacher said', or

'The disciple asked', and one is reminded of Nietzsche's formulae in *Also sprach Zarathustra*. In the succeeding volumes the essays often have a more anecdotal form, even incorporate short conversations, and take up, too, incidents from Strindberg's life, though the range of subject-matter continues to be just as wide, with such titles as *King Lear's Wife, What is Science?, Life of Jesus*. The index of the complete *Blue Books* conjures up the image of that kind of encyclopaedia for which, in its moral informativeness, our ancestors a hundred years ago had such a partiality. In the *Blue Books*, indeed, Strindberg sounds much deeper notes than the merely sententious. For instance, in *A New Blue Book* (*En Ny Blå Bok*), the meditation on Sorrow (*Sorgen*) lets the reader divine the depth and intensity of his love for Harriet Bosse, for whom, in her absence, he carries on a kind of spiritual cult. 'The greatest moment of love resembles that of death; the closed eyes, the pallor of death, the loss of consciousness.'[1] Yet the tone is often one of fierce diatribe and of contempt for mankind, a continuation of the manner of *Black Banners* in its fulmination against the vices and hypocrisy of the world and, more especially, of Sweden. Equally Strindberg reveals how he despises the sciences of which he writes, for instance biology and philology, just as much as the arts, in comparison with religion, which alone will save man's soul: the scientists, indeed, are referred to as 'magicians and charlatans'. Strindberg's own brand of religion included by now the ragtag and bobtail of various sects and faiths, still strongly coloured by Swedenborg, whose *Diarium Spirituale* inspired this, his own Occult Diary; what is most important, he now maintains, is to believe; and with the credulousness

[1] *S.S.* XLVII, 776.

already made manifest in *Inferno*, and now become much more obstinate, he interprets knockings, cramps, and other such signs, as occult messages, warnings from the Powers against this or that evil action or thought: even if such warnings are directly caused by human agency, they are none the less fulfilling a divine purpose. In this way Strindberg opens up vast fields for occult intervention, so that even the most ordinary objects take on a supernatural aura. An interesting light on his mentality in these matters is cast by an incident reported by the famous artist and humorist Albert Engström,[1] when Strindberg, rejecting the common-sense explanation of the pressing of a certain pair of trousers, in favour of his own mystical interpretation, burst out: 'You are impossible. You are only a realist, and therefore nothing happens to you.' There is here a suggestion of quite deliberate mystification. The complex psychological portrait of the author which is built up throughout the pages of these *Blue Books* gives these volumes their only enduring value. Not least revealing are the blind spots, but Strindberg furnishes also that detailed analysis of himself and others that made the autobiographical works so fascinating. He had described the first *Blue Book* as 'the synthesis of my life', referring to the contents rather than to the form; but it is difficult to pass that definition when one is confronted with this web of speculations and doubts, bitter regrets, moods of resignation, grievances, reproaches, and uneasy exculpations, shot through at the same time with so much real pity and so much genuine suffering.

[1] See Albert Engström, *Strindberg och jag* (Stockholm 1923).

CONCLUSION

BY reason of the almost irrelevant accident of the centenary of Strindberg's birth, the arc lights of public interest have just been turned, rather suddenly, upon him in this country. Through the medium of the wireless, the press, and even of the London stage, the name of this Swedish writer, who, by the uninterested many, was so often dismissed as 'that Norwegian lunatic', has for a moment become something *actuel* and therefore interesting. It would be a pity if Strindberg's interest for the English should be limited to this transitory, squib-like appearance, if knowledge of him and understanding for him should not persist in some more permanent and less superficial form. It seems probable that the previous general ignorance of his work in this country can be attributed, at least in part, to prejudices which have been fostered by the very enthusiasm of some of those few people who have been anxious to launch him here as a prophet, for in this way Strindberg, like Nietzsche, has been invested with the crankiness of his disciples, and for cranks there prevails in England a profound and on the whole healthy distaste. But in fact Strindberg cannot fairly be termed a mere crank, nor does he compel attention as a prophet. It is as a writer that he deserves to be studied, while his personality, however irritating and, in certain aspects, even repellent, has the fascination of a complicated problem in human psychology. Furthermore, knowledge of Strindberg's life and experiences, or rather of his own individual reactions to those experiences, does help considerably—more with him than with most people—to explain the works to the reader. There is nothing particularly esoteric in Strindberg's thesis, and the alleged incomprehensibility of his works can be, and in England has been, greatly exaggerated. Strindberg's main ideas, as expressed in his works and outlined in this book, seem, as ideas, fairly simple, however complicated may be the illustrative examples chosen by him, and however surprising the juxtaposition of mutually contradictory standpoints. Indeed, Strindberg may more justly be criticised for the repetitiveness of his opinions than for their inherent obscurity; certainly never, or almost never, for lack of clarity in expressing them.

The myth of incomprehensibility, one may suspect, derives, in England, from quite another aspect of Strindberg's work, that is, from the often or generally pessimistic tone of his writings, which resounds in the tragic violence of the conflicts and the violent reactions of his characters. Perhaps it is this tragic vehemence which strikes the English reader most forcibly, and repels him, unless or until he can adjust himself to the values implied. Partly it is Strindberg's own sharpness of response and his fierce vitality that explain the vehemence, partly one may conclude that his aggressive emphasis on certain ideas betrays and underlines his inward doubts, both of himself and his beliefs, so that the overtones in the abuse and the slam of the banged door on the stage are the author's own anguished whispers and subdued searchings of the heart. The tragic tone, however, so the reader will argue, remains; but this charge of unduly tragic outlook can be levelled against much of Scandinavian literature as a whole, more specifically against Norwegian and Swedish literature. Strindberg is not 'gloomier' than many other

Northern authors. The German, so often apparently humourless himself, does not reject foreign literature on the score of 'gloom'. No doubt this explains the easy success in Germany, many years ago, of some of Strindberg's worse efforts. Yet there is, one may think, implicit in the German acceptance an underrating or ignoring of Strindberg's own peculiar humour and sense of irony, which are there for the English reader to find and enjoy, though so often distorted or obscured by clumsy translations (Strindberg's language at the best of times almost defies rendering into English). Because Strindberg's sense of humour is not an English one, that does not mean that it has not a positive, Swedish, character, a fact which holds good for many other Swedish writers as well. The *snaps*-drinking lumberjack of Northern Sweden, up against the rigours and monotony of the endless snow-covered forests, must of necessity develop a different kind of humour from that of the beer-swilling yokels of Shakespeare's Warwickshire. Thus the humour in *The People of Hemsö* may be coarse and at times grim; nevertheless it is humour.

Certain Swedish critics of Strindberg, of whom Heidenstam was really the first, have called him a barbarian, and have dwelt on his savage strength and uncontrolled moods. This interpretation deliberately leaves out of account the hypersensitive temperament and in many ways sophisticated responses of the author, a sophistication which is often revealed in irony, and thus rejects what to many of his readers must be his greatest fascination—the combination of primitive, dynamic vitality and poetic imagination with a subtle awareness of all the discordant and conflicting claims of life, as they arise in modern society. Strindberg does not, like his much better known contemporary Ibsen, busy himself with projecting contemporary social problems *qua* social problems on the stage. One may say that his canvas would have been a more varied one if he had done so, yet, through this, his plays, even if more abstract, are less dependent on matters of merely topical interest. Like Ibsen, on the other hand, Strindberg was intent on stripping the mask from hypocrisy: and against the faultless workmanship and extraordinarily intelligent, though sometimes over-schematic, art of the Norwegian, his most positive quality is clearly revealed by contrast; that most positive quality is his fluidity.

SELECT BIBLIOGRAPHY

A. Collected Works

Samlade Skrifter av August Strindberg (55 vols. Bonnier's, Stockholm, 1911–21).

B. Letters

August Strindbergs Brev (Stockholm, 1948). In progress.

Från Fjärdingen till Blå Tornet, ett Brevurval 1870–1912 (ed. T. Eklund, 1946).

Strindbergs Brev till Harriet Bosse (1932).

C. Writings about Strindberg in English

J. Bulman, *Strindberg and Shakespeare* (1933).

G. A. Campbell, *Strindberg* ('Great Lives' series, 1933).

C. E. W. L. Dahlström, *Strindberg's Dramatic Expressionism* (1930).

V. J. McGill, *August Strindberg, the Bedevilled Viking* (1930).

H. V. E. Palmblad, *Strindberg's Conception of History* (1927).

E. Sprigge, *The Strange Life of August Strindberg* (1949).

F. Strindberg, *Marriage with Genius* (translation of *Lieb, Leid und Zeit*, 1937).

A. J. Upvall, *August Strindberg, a Psychoanalytic Study* (1920).

D. Other Writings about Strindberg

(Except where otherwise stated, these writings are in Swedish.)

W. A. Berendsohn, *Strindbergs-problem* (1946).

F. Böök, *Svenska Litteraturens Historia*, III, 86 ff.

V. Børge, *Kvinden i Strindbergs Liv* (1936) (Danish).

G. M. C. Brandes, 'August Strindberg' in *Germanisch-Romanische Monatsschrift*, VI, 321 ff. (German).

G. Castrén, *Illustrerad Svensk Litteraturhistoria* (ed. H. Schück and K. Warburg), VII.

T. Eklund, 'Strindbergs Verksamhet som Publicist 1869–1880' in *Samlaren*, X, N.S., 142 ff.

T. Eklund, *Tjänstekvinnans Son* (1948).

N. Erdmann, *August Strindberg* (2 vols., 1920).

A. Falck, *Fem År med Strindberg* (1935).

Fanny Falkner, *August Strindberg i Blå Tornet* (1921).

224

BIBLIOGRAPHY

O. Hansson, 'Erinnerungen an August Strindberg' in *Neue Rund schau* for 1912, II, 1536ff., 1724ff. (German).

E. Hedén, *Strindberg, en Ledtråd vid Studiet av hans Verk* (1921).

H. Jacobsen, *Strindberg i Firsernes København* (1948) (Danish).

H. Jacobsen, *Strindberg och hans första Hustru* (1948) (Swedish translation from the Danish).

K. Jaspers, *Strindberg und Van Gogh* (1922) (German).

M. Lamm, *Strindberg* (2 vols. 1940–2).

M. Lamm, *Strindberg och Makterna* (1936).

M. Lamm, *Strindbergs Dramer* (2 vols. 1924–6).

S. Linder, *Ibsen, Strindberg och andra* (1936).

A. Lundegård, *Några Strindbergsminnen knutna till en handfull brev* (1920).

B. Mörner, *Den Strindberg jag känt* (1924).

J. Mortensen, *Från Röda Rummet till Sekelskiftet* (2 vols. 1918–19).

J. Mortensen, *Strindberg som jag minnes honom* (1931).

G. Ollén, *Strindberg's Dramatik* (1948).

A. Paul, *Min Strindbergsbok* (2nd edition, 1930).

A. v. Philp and N. Hartzell, *Strindbergs Systrar berätta* (1926).

S. Rahmer, *August Strindberg, eine pathologische Studie* (1907) (German).

C. L. Schleich, *Erinnerungen an Strindberg* (1917) (German).

G. Schmid, 'Strindbergs naturwissenschaftliche Schriften' in *Neue Rundschau*, LXXVI (1918) (German).

Karin Smirnoff, *Strindbergs första Hustru* (2nd edition, 1926).

G. Uddgren, *August Strindberg* (1912).

G. Uddgren, *Andra Boken om Strindberg* (1912).

R. Zetterlund, *Bibliografiska Anteckningar om August Strindberg* (1913).

F. Translations of Strindberg's Writings into English

i. *Series*

1. *The Plays of August Strindberg* (translated by E. Björkman, 1912–13). CONTENTS: I, Dream Play, Link, Dance of Death I and II; II, Creditors, Pariah, There are Crimes and Crimes, Miss Julia, Stronger; III, Swanwhite, Simoom, Debit and Credit, Thunderstorm, Advent, After the Fire; IV, Bridal Crown, Spook Sonata, First Warning, Gustav Vasa.

2. *Plays of August Strindberg* (E. Oland, W. Oland and V. S. L. Howard, 1913–14). CONTENTS: I, Father, Countess Julie, Outlaw, Stronger; II, Comrades, Facing Death, Pariah, Easter; III, Lucky Peter; IV, Swanwhite, Advent, Storm.

BIBLIOGRAPHY

3. *Plays of August Strindberg* (H. B. Samuel, 1914). CONTENTS:
   I, Miss Julia; II, Stronger Woman, Motherly Love; III,
   Creditor; IV, Pariah, Simoom; V, Comrades.
4. *Scandinavian Classics*, published by the American-Scandinavian
   Foundation. Vol. IV (1915), Master Olof (translation from
   the prose version of 1872 by E. Björkman); Vol. XXX (n.d.),
   Sweden's Best Stories, including Autumn, Stone Man, Half
   Sheet of Paper.
5. Publications of the Anglo-Swedish Foundation:
       (a) *Easter and Other Plays* (E. Classen, J. B. Fagan, C. D.
   Locock, E. Palmstierna, 1929). CONTENTS: Easter, Dance
   of Death I and II, Ghost Sonata, Dream Play.
       (b) *Lucky Peter s Travels and Other Plays* (E. Classen, C. D.
   Locock, C. Napier, E. Sprigge, 1930). CONTENTS: Lucky
   Peter's Travels, Father, Lady Julie, Playing with Fire, Bond.
       (c) *Master Olof and Other Plays* (J. Bulman, C. D. Locock,
   1931). CONTENTS: Master Olof, Gustav Vasa, Erik XIV,
   Saga of the Folkungs.
       (d) *The Road to Damascus, a Trilogy* (G. Rawson, 1932).

ii. *Single Volumes*

6. *The Father* (translated by N. Erichsen, 1899).
7. *The Creditor* (F. J. Ziegler, 1910).
8. *The Confession of a Fool* (E. Schleussner, 1912).
9. *The Inferno* (C. Field, 1912).
10. *Legends* (anonymous, 1912).
11. *Lucky Pehr* (V. S. Howard, 1912).
12. *By the Open Sea [I Havsbandet]* (E. Schleussner, 1913).
13. *Easter and Stories* (V. S. Howard, 1913).
14. *The Growth of a Soul* (C. Field, 1913).
15. *Historical Miniatures [Historiska Miniatvrer]* (C. Field, 1913).
16. *In Midsummer Days and Other Tales* (E. Schleussner, 1913).
17. *Married, Twenty Stories* (E. Schleussner, 1913).
18. *The Red Room* (E. Schleussner, 1913).
19. *The Son of a Servant* (C. Field, 1913).
20. *Zones of the Spirit [En Blå Bok]* (C. Field, 1913).
21. *Fair Haven and Foul Strand [Fagervik och Skamsund]* (anon. 1913).
22. *The Martyr of Stockholm [På Gott och Ont]*[1] (C. Field, 1914).
23. *The German Lieutenant and Other Stories* (C. Field, 1915).
24. *Advent* (C. Field, 1922).
25. *Tales [Sagor]* (L. J. Potts, 1930).

[1] From *Svenska Öden och Äventyr*, III.

INDEX

[The main entries are in bold figures. Strindberg's works are listed alphabetically under the heading Strindberg, August: WRITINGS.]*

INDEX

Iceland, Strindberg's interest in, 16, 19, 21, 95
Inferno Crisis, Strindberg's so-called, **54 ff.**, 200 ff.
Intima Teatern, **79 ff.**, 83, **213 ff.**
Italy and the Italians, 41 n.

Jacobsen, H., 24 n., 225
Jäderin, Axel, 16 f.
Japan and the Japanese, 85
Jaspers, Karl, 35, 55, 61, 225
Jesus Christ, 18, 33, 218; see also religion
Josephson, Joseph, 16 f.
Juel, Dagny, 48 n.

Kempis, Thomas à, 57
Key, Ellen, 77 f., 172
Kierkegaard, Søren Aaby, 22
Kléen, Emil, 159
Knorring, Sophie v., 148
Kotzebue, August v., 147
Krohg, Christian, 48
Kymmendö, 19, 29, 161

Lafontaine, August Heinrich Julius, 147
Lagerlöf, Selma Ottilina Lovisa, 76
Lamm, Axel, 12 f., 14 f., 22, 24, 193
Lamm, Martin, 1 n., 46 n., 225
Lancet (periodical), 25
Landquist, J., 1 n.
Lassalle, Ferdinand, 41
Levertin, Oscar, 87, 185, 211
Lidforss, Bengt, 48, 52 n., 63 n.
Lindquist, J., 42 n.
London, 50
Lund, 59, 60 ff., 66, 67, 79 n., 122 f., 187
Lundegård, Axel, 24 n., 42 n., 225
Lundin, Claes, 31, 209
Luther, Martin and lutheranism, 9, 73 n., 95 ff., 133; see also religion

Maeterlinck, Maurice Polydore Marie Bernard, 72, 133, 135 f., 140
Marholm, Laura (*pseudonym*), 47 f.,
Marx, Carl, 180
McCarthy, Justin, 50
McGill, V. J., 224
Molière (*pseudonym*), 125, 213
Mörk, Jakob Henrik, 146 f.
Mörner, Birger, 24 n., 47, 52
Mortensen, Johan, 63, 66
Munch, Edvard, 48
music, Strindberg and, 3, 6, 83 f.

Nansen, Peter, 44 n.
Nasby, Petroleum V. (*pseudonym*), 23
naturalism and naturalists in literature, 108 f., 113, 115 f., 160 f., 170, 184, 190, 216; see also Théâtre Libre *and* Zola
Neijber (family), 2
Nietzsche, Friedrich Wilhelm, and his doctrines, 41 f., 54 n., 56 n., 57, 86, 112 f., 164, 218
Nobel prize for literature, 87 f.
Norling, Johan Olof, and his wife, 1, 7, 8 f.
Norway and the Norwegians, 32, 86 n., 150; see also Bjørnson, Ibsen
Nyblom, Carl Rupert, 15

Œhlenschläger, Adam Gottlob, 15, 105
Offenbach, Jacques, 10
Ollén, G., 225
Owen, Samuel, 3

Painting, Strindberg's interest in, 83 n.
Palmblad, V. E., 224
Paris, 32, 50, 56 ff., 60, 202, 216 *et passim*
Parker, Theodore, 10 f., 18, 21, 40, 94
Paul, Adolf, 46 n., 48, 225

229

INDEX